Restoring the City on a Hill

U.S. History and Civics in America's Schools

EDITORS

Chris Sinacola and Jamie Gass

PIONEER INSTITUTE
PUBLIC POLICY RESEARCH

October 2023

PIONEER INSTITUTE
PUBLIC POLICY RESEARCH

Pioneer's **mission** is to develop and communicate dynamic ideas that advance prosperity and a vibrant civic life in Massachusetts and beyond.

Pioneer's **vision of success** is a state and nation where our people can prosper and our society thrive because we enjoy world-class options in education, healthcare, transportation, and economic opportunity, and where our government is limited, accountable, and transparent.

Pioneer **values** an America where our citizenry is well-educated and willing to test our beliefs based on facts and the free exchange of ideas, and committed to liberty, personal responsibility, and free enterprise.

CONTENTS

Ignoring U.S. History at Our Peril

State must make good on requirement for history instruction and testing

By William Weld and Tom Birmingham

In 1993, we collaborated on the landmark Massachusetts Education Reform Act, arguably the most far-reaching and consequential state legislation signed into law in a generation. Winning support for any such law requires significant compromise, but one thing that the executive and legislative branches agreed upon was the importance of K–12 education students knowing about our nation's history and civic duties.

The 1993 law explicitly required instruction about the Declaration of Independence, *The Federalist Papers*, and the U.S. Constitution. We also made passage of a U.S. history test a high school graduation requirement.

Sadly, subsequent generations of political leaders have not shared our view of the importance of U.S. history. It is now becoming an afterthought in too many of our public schools.

The Founding Fathers believed that to exercise the rights and privileges of citizenship, Americans had to understand our history and its seminal documents. They also saw it as the role of public schools to pass on what James Madison called "the political religion of the nation" to its children.

As the great educational standards expert E.D. Hirsch, Jr. has said, "The aim of schooling was not just to Americanize the immigrants, but also to Americanize the Americans."

Without education as a unifying force, the Founders feared that the new nation itself might dissolve. After all, internal dissension had brought down every previous republic.

According to Professor Hirsch, the public school curriculum should be based on acquiring wide, substantive background knowledge, not just learning how to learn. This belief is diametrically opposed to the view held by too many education policymakers that the main purpose of public education should be to prepare students for the workforce.

As it turns out, the evidence is strong that students who receive a broad liberal arts education tend to do better financially than those taught a narrower curriculum focused on training students for a job.

The role of public schools in creating citizens capable of informed participation in American democracy is particularly important in a pluralistic society like ours. Unlike so many others, our country was not based upon a state religion, ancient boundaries, or bloodlines, but on a shared system of ideas, principles, and beliefs.

On the heels of their experience as British subjects, our Founders envisioned public schools would create an aristocracy based on merit and talent; a nation of strivers in which hard work and intelligence—not birthright—would determine who succeeds.

When Horace Mann, the father of American public education, took the helm of the new Massachusetts Board of Education in the 1830s, he too believed that public education's most important role was to prepare students to be active participants in our nation's democracy. When Mann founded the first system of public schools, he envisioned them safeguarding democracy by educating students in its principles.

In 2009, the administration of Massachusetts Governor Deval Patrick eliminated the requirement that students pass a

U.S. history test to graduate from high school. The administration made that move before the test ever had a chance to be administered.

At the time, the Patrick Administration cited the estimated $2.4 million that would be needed to administer the test. In a multibillion-dollar state budget, such a modest sum surely could have been found had there been a sincere desire to implement the test. That remains true today.

Since the demise of the U.S. history graduation requirement, history and civics education have been sidelined in Massachusetts, especially in urban school districts. Entire history departments have been eliminated, and it's common for the history courses that remain to be taught by teachers whose expertise is in other subjects.

English, math, science, and social studies — including history — are all important. We should not sacrifice one to improve performance in another. Yet, without reinstating passage of a U.S. history test as a graduation requirement, there will be no way to measure student progress in history and civics, or to ensure that local school districts affirmatively support history departments.

Unless we again make U.S. history, civics, and the documents that form the basis of our republic a priority, we risk a generation that will be unable to fully participate in America's democracy. And it won't take many such generations before the very republic itself is placed at risk.

■ ■ ■

Former Massachusetts governor William Weld is an attorney in Boston. The late Thomas Birmingham, a former president of the state Senate, was coauthor of the landmark 1993 Massachusetts Education Reform Act.

Why Study History?
The Case of Winston Churchill

By Paul Reid

In 1953 Winston Churchill told an American student: "Young man, study history, study history. In history lie all the secrets of statecraft."

The young man in question, James Humes, took Churchill's advice to heart, and went on to become a presidential speechwriter and historian. Of course, when an outsized historical figure such as Winston Churchill suggests a course of action, it likely pays to listen.

And yet, what exactly did Churchill mean by that advice? As usual with Churchill, there is more here than first meets the eye. Did Churchill mean that in history lie all the secrets of practicing statecraft? Was this a case of an old politician advising a young man with political ambitions to study history in order to perfect his craft? I think not.

A perusal of Churchill's written and spoken words — and his actions — over seven decades on the subject of history reveals that he believed every citizen in a democracy, in order to evaluate practitioners of statecraft, must study history.

Otherwise, the citizen can be sold a bill of goods by a clever or unscrupulous politician or, what is far worse, be enslaved by a tyrant who distorts and falsifies history with wicked intent. Think of Hitler. Churchill certainly did.

Churchill's advice was a warning: Ignorance of history on the part of the citizenry breeds consequences, and likely bad consequences, for civil liberties, even for personal safety. Churchill's advice was not a variation on George Santayana's maxim that those who forget history are doomed to repeat it. Churchill certainly agreed with Santayana, but he was saying something else to young Humes: Those who study history are less likely to become victims of history, are less likely to be gulled by those who seek — for good or ill — political power.

That sentiment is cited in one way or another by history teachers on the first day of a high school history or civics class: We're here to become better and better-informed citizens. To do so requires far more than memorizing a catalogue of names, dates, and events. It requires the ability to critically analyze and interpret those names, dates, and events. That is the essence of Churchill's advice.

To ponder and discuss Churchill's advice to Humes requires at least a modest background in … history. To evaluate Churchill's advice requires at least a cursory understanding of Churchill and the role he played on the world stage for seven decades. That is, to even begin to discuss the first paragraph in this essay requires a sense of history. To complete the circuit—Churchill's advice, discussion of it, analysis, refutation, or affirmation—requires the ability to apply reason and opinion informed by history.

Churchill made his living as an author. What did he write? History. Multivolume histories of World War I, World War II, a biography of his luminous ancestor, John Churchill, the Duke of Marlborough, and a history of the English-speaking peoples.

He was curious about everything — new technologies, political and economic trends, geography, language (well, the English language anyway), ancient history, modern history. He predicted genetic engineering of crops, and even humans, in the 1930s.

He was the father of the battle tank and was ridiculed by experts when he proposed it. Naysayers called the tank "Winston's folly," until it helped win World War I. He predicted throughout the 1930s that Adolf Hitler was intent on conquering Europe, from Moscow to the North Sea. For that, too, he was ridiculed.

He based that prediction on a careful reading of Hitler's *Mein Kampf*, wherein Hitler told the world exactly what he intended to do, and how. Hitler's book was his blueprint, right there for all to see. Few saw.

Churchill was self-taught. He never graduated from college. His appetite for the written word was astounding—all of Shakespeare, the historians Macaulay and Gibbon, Dr. Johnson, Karl Marx, Kipling, Mark Twain, Nietzsche, Abraham Lincoln's speeches, General Grant's memoirs, the Hornblower adventure novels, Dickens, and much more, along with at least six newspapers each day. He did so because he loved doing so.

Churchill also enjoyed Marx Brothers movies and Donald Duck cartoons. These were his stimulants; they got his intellectual juices flowing; they offered sensation and propelled him to action. History, for Churchill, was not dead, but alive with possibilities.

He told friends and family that the cornerstone of his interest in history was his infatuation with the human condition. He believed that history is far more than a repository of dusty documents, dates, and artifacts. History is the unfolding of mankind's story, the sum of our actions.

Churchill's advice to young Humes can be seen as a variation of "Know thyself." He believed that if we, as citizens, do not know our collective story, if we do not or cannot reference our collective memory, we cannot know ourselves as a nation, as a people. Our character traits, and the ability to decipher them, are revealed not through mathematics or pure science or engineering, but through history.

Yet Churchill once told an audience: "History, with its flickering lamp stumbles along the trail of the past, trying to reconstruct its scenes, to revive its echoes, and kindle with pale gleams the passion of former days." That is a cautionary phrase, perhaps one that should not be told to young history students on their first day of class.

Churchill meant that historical truths do not reveal themselves with the absolute clarity of mathematical or scientific truth. History is shadowy, rife with hard-to-fathom motives and passions. It challenges us. That is why Churchill loved it. He loved a challenge above all else.

History demands critical thinking. To teach it by rote — by listing dates, winners and losers of battles, famous documents — is to not teach it at all. To teach history effectively the teacher must employ the novelist's tools of plot, narrative pace, character, tension, suspense. Churchill hated his history classes as a young boy at Harrow because, he later realized, his teachers reduced heroic people and events to mere names and dates. The heart of the story was lost. As was any wisdom or guidance the story might contain.

Churchill once told an American audience, "As history unfolds itself, by strange and unpredictable paths, we have little control over the future and no control at all over the past."

Does this imply a certain pessimism, a certain resignation, on Churchill's part? No. Churchill stressed to friends, family, and countrymen, over long dinners and in speeches in the House of Commons, that while we have no control over the past, the past can inform our decisions in the present. Those decisions and their consequences will beget the future.

Along with historical context and consequences, Churchill saw the beauty of — and the enigmatic irony of — contingency in history. No other academic discipline is so rife with what-if scenarios.

But what-if questions can have real, practical, even mortal significance. In Britain, in 1940, it was no parlor game to ask: What if Hitler throws his armies across the English Channel to Britain? Many in Britain believed Hitler would do so.

But Churchill knew that the Royal Navy, vastly larger than the German navy, would destroy any armada; Germany was — historically — a land power, never a sea power. Sustained by his historical knowledge, Churchill believed no German invasion would take place, and accordingly sent men and tanks to Egypt.

Many in Britain were appalled, but Churchill was proven correct. No German invasion ever took place. Churchill believed that Britain, behind its North Sea moat, would survive and prevail. In the end, he led the West to victory against the criminal wickedness of Nazi Germany.

Churchill wrote millions of words and earned millions of dollars doing so. He was awarded the Nobel Prize for Literature. Had he never spent a single day in Parliament or led Britain in World War II he would be known today as one of the premier historians of the twentieth century. Had he never written a single book, he would be known as an intrepid war correspondent. Had he never been a journalist he would be known as a talented painter. He was, indeed, a Renaissance man.

A cynic, with a modest knowledge of Churchill and twentieth-century history, might ask, why is Churchill's opinion on the value of studying history worth anything? We live in an age when everyone is entitled to his or her opinion. But not all opinions have value; some opinions are both baseless and dangerous. Absent sound knowledge and critical thinking, such ideas can take root in the public consciousness.

More hazardous to our collective intellectual health than a cynic who begrudges Churchill the validity of his opinion, is the person who reads this essay and asks, who is Winston Churchill? Who is Martin Luther King? Who is Susan B. Anthony? What is the Supreme Court? Where is the Pacific Ocean? Or one who asks a most unsettling question: Why bother to vote?

In 1929, Churchill told an audience: "How strange it is that the past is so little understood and so quickly forgotten. We live in the most thoughtless of ages. Every day, headlines and short views. I have tried to drag history up a little nearer to our own times in case it should be helpful as a guide in present difficulties."

Almost a century later Churchill's words ring true for our times. Our print newspapers are dying. The internet resembles the gunfight at the OK Corral on a vast scale — everybody shooting, few taking aim. Yet the news of the day still demands critical thinking. Possible consequences and contingencies need to be put into historical context by engaged citizens. Are we doing so? Time — and history — will tell.

Churchill often spoke of history in metaphorical terms, using Mark Twain's *Life on the Mississippi* as one of his sources. In his memoir Twain writes a marvelous chapter about learning to become a riverboat pilot under the tutelage of a curmudgeonly old pilot, who told him that you learn the river by feeling it. The spring thaw in Wisconsin could result in dangerous water at Memphis; an ice dam on the Ohio River could mean low water on the Mississippi. To know the river, a pilot had to know its history.

That, Churchill liked to tell friends over brandy and cigars, was how human history worked. History swirls around us, carries us forward on its currents, steers us toward shoals that we best learn how to pass safely by. History is not mileposts that point the way; history is in flux, always, like the river. Diligent citizens — and their political leaders — must understand that.

Lifelong, Churchill did his bit for the cause of history. He made history; he wrote history; he loved to parse history. Today, our leaders must do their bit to ensure that history is taught in all public schools, that students are tested and that today's young citizens are prepared for the challenges of tomorrow's world. The lamp of history, even with its pale gleams, can help them light their way. The alternative is to carry no lamp at all.

■   ■   ■

Paul Reid is coauthor with William Manchester of The Last Lion: Defender of the Realm, Winston Spencer Churchill — 1940–1965.

CHAPTER 1

Shortchanging the Future

The Crisis of History and Civics in American Schools

By Robert Pondiscio, Gilbert T. Sewall,
and Dr. Sandra Stotsky

*"History by apprising [citizens] of the past will enable them to judge
of the future; it will avail them of the experience of other times and
other nations; it will qualify them as judges of the actions and designs of men; it will enable them to know ambition under every
disguise it may assume; and knowing it, to defeat its views."*

– THOMAS JEFFERSON, *NOTES ON THE STATE OF VIRGINIA*,
QUERY 14, 1781

Introduction

The collective grasp of basic United States history and civics
among American students is alarmingly weak. Beyond dispirit-
ing test results on the National Assessment of Educational Progress (NAEP) and other measures, poor performance in history
and civics portends a decay of the knowledge, skills, and disposi-
tions needed for a lifetime of active, engaged citizenship.

The reasons for this decline are many. The amount of time devoted to U.S. history in K–12 education has demonstrably shrunk
over time. Further, demands to make curriculum more inclusive
have led schools and teachers to dwell on social history, race, and

gender in ways that distort the nation's historical narrative.

These changes are in turn reflected in textbooks and teaching materials used in social studies classrooms. Problems with teacher training and qualification compound the problem, leaving teachers poorly equipped to arrest the decline in history and civics.

Past efforts to arrest or reverse the decline, however well intentioned, have had little impact. Attempts to create national history standards have failed, and great caution must be exercised before further efforts are made to write or impose such standards.

Instead, states should consider adopting highly rated sets of standards in history and social science such as those that — at least until recent years — have been used in South Carolina, California, and Massachusetts.

In addition, states should consider using the U.S. Citizenship Test as a requirement for students to graduate from a public high school, be admitted to a public college, or be eligible for a Pell Grant or other public funds.

Is the Study of United States History on the Wrong Side of History?

When Americans speak of the crisis in education, we typically cite the poor performance of children in reading, mathematics, and science. Compared to our students' grasp of foundational ideas in history and civics, however, reading, mathematics, and science are pillars of strength.

While history teachers with low academic expectations have contributed to the unsatisfactory level of historical knowledge among high school graduates, a much greater factor is the steady decay of the content of the history curriculum, the decline of its standing within K–12 education, and the methods teachers use to convey hollowed-out content.

History lessons and civics education too often celebrate diversity and bolster student self-esteem rather than ensure a deep understanding of the past and the responsibilities citizens have in a representative form of self-government.

In 1983, the landmark education report *A Nation at Risk*

memorably stated that "if an unfriendly foreign power had attempted to impose on America the mediocre educational performance that exists today, we might well have viewed it as an act of war."

Our earliest commentators on the public purpose of education might have viewed our present neglect of civics and history as an act of treason.

As E.D. Hirsch, Jr. observed in *The Making of Americans*, eighteenth- and nineteenth-century contributors to the nation's political structure saw schools as the main hope for the preservation of democratic ideals and the republic. As James Madison said, "The advancement and diffusion of knowledge is the only guardian of true liberty."[1]

Today, we view the goals of education largely through an economic lens and are too often narrowly concerned with "college and career readiness" and economic competitiveness.

Yet, the neglect of a commonly understood heritage and the failure to cultivate civic values breed cynicism, distrust, and the decidedly un-American idea that ordinary citizens lack agency to manage their own affairs.

History has come to be seen as secondary in importance to literacy and mathematics. Textbooks are declining in importance and quality. Dubious strategies and activities, cloaked with benign or positive attributes, make it difficult for parents to understand the damage done to the history and social studies curriculum.

Further, today's teachers were educated in an era of diminished emphasis on history and civics.

There have been many well-conceived attempts at reform and several examples of first-rate curricular and pedagogical approaches. However, none has had any discernible impact on trends in K–12 history and civics curriculum or overall student achievement.

In this opening chapter, we review changes in the curriculum in the past half-century and suggest how alterations in content occurred. An explanation of the role of state guidelines, regulations, and statutes leads to a discussion of the placement of U.S.

history in the curriculum, the problems and limitations of teacher qualifications, and deficiencies in current instructional materials.

Finally, we discuss how national and state standards have contributed to the problems of history and civics education today.

What National Tests in History and Civics Tell Us

Historical illiteracy among the nation's high school students is not new. It has been discussed and lamented by eminent intellectuals and historians from George Santayana to Richard Hofstadter. It has also been documented by the NAEP history tests given to students in grades 4, 8, and 12 from 1986 to the present.

NAEP history tests

On the 1986 grade 12 test, for example, 60 percent of students did not know that the purpose of *The Federalist Papers* was to promote ratification of the U.S. Constitution in New York State; 60 percent failed to recognize the purpose of Lincoln's Emancipation Proclamation; 40 percent were not familiar with the concept of checks and balances; and a third could not identify the Declaration of Independence.

"Many [students]," one study commented at the time, "lack a clear understanding of the fundamental document that defines the organization and powers of the federal government, as well as the rights and liberties of citizens."[2]

Scores through the 1990s made clear that a lack of historical knowledge extended into elementary and middle schools. In 1995, over 80 percent of students in grades 4, 8, and 12 failed to achieve the Proficient level that, according to NAEP, demonstrates "solid academic performance."[3]

"More than half of America's high school seniors," the *New York Times* wrote in 1995, "do not know basic facts about American history…"[4]

On the 2006 NAEP history test, only 13 percent of seniors scored Proficient, while over half failed to score at the Basic level. Scores in 2010 were unchanged: Fourth graders could not explain why Lincoln was important. Perhaps most alarming, 98 percent of graduating seniors could not explain the importance of *Brown v. Board of Education*, the landmark U.S. Supreme Court ruling that led to the integration of America's public schools.[5]

NAEP civics tests

The NAEP civics tests document a similar collapse of civics literacy. Scores for grades 8 and 12 were stagnant from 1998 to 2006. Just 43 percent of the grade 12 test-takers could describe federalism in American government.[6]

The 2010 civics results revealed serious and growing deficiencies in the high school curriculum when compared to those from 1998 and before.[7] The percentage of students who said they studied the United States Constitution during the school year fell from 72 percent in 2006 to 67 percent in 2010.

Impact of higher education on history and civics knowledge

College seems to add little to students' understanding or appreciation of history and civics. Reviews of college programs by the National Association of Scholars and others indicate fewer general requirements and more emphasis on race, class, and gender.

In 2006, the Intercollegiate Studies Institute (ISI) gave approximately 14,000 college freshmen and seniors at 50 colleges nationwide a 60-question multiple-choice exam on fundamental knowledge of America's history and institutions. The average freshman scored 51.7 percent, and the average senior scored 53.2 percent.[8]

In a 2007 test of another 14,000 college freshmen and seniors, the average freshman scored 50.4 percent, and the average senior scored 54.2 percent.

In 2008, ISI widened the field of respondents to adults to measure the independent impact of college on the acquisition of civics knowledge. A sample of 2,508 American adults was given a 33-question basic civics test. The average college graduate scored 57 percent, correctly answering only four questions more than the average high school graduate.

A disturbing trend and implications

Poor performance on NAEP assessments over decades has raised alarms, particularly since long-term voting trends in national elections for young adults demonstrate that a low level of civics literacy correlates with a low level of civic participation.

Voter turnout among Americans ages 18–24 in the 2010 midterm election was 21.3 percent, down from 25.4 percent in 1974, according to the 2010 United States Census Current Population Survey, November Supplement.[9]

Such figures may have seen some improvement a decade later, when the Census estimates that about 27 percent of voters between the ages of 18 and 29 cast a ballot in the 2022 midterm elections.

Despite such scattered signs of hope, however, the long-term effects of current K–12 history and civics curricula in public schools across the nation are not merely disappointing, but profoundly disturbing.

Changes in the History Curriculum

Three factors have altered the content of the K–12 history curriculum and reduced the time students spend on it:

- An emphasis on modern U.S. history
- Added social content
- A new emphasis on world history

Curriculum narrowing and the compression of U.S. history

In elementary schools, history and civics education take a back seat to language arts and math. A large-scale 2005 study showed only 5.2 percent of third-grade class time spent on social studies.[10]

High schools often mandate the teaching of world history, limiting the time spent on U.S. history. In some schools, a thematic approach compresses U.S. history and leaves gaps in knowledge. The War of 1812, settlement of the American West, and the Industrial Revolution may remain in textbooks but receive little attention. And few public schools require students to read a complete history book or write a serious history term paper.

Alignment of American history with identity politics

Many teachers today focus on social history, race, and gender in ways that distort historical narratives. In the late 1970s and early 1980s, Frances FitzGerald in *The New Yorker* and C. Vann Woodward in *The New Republic* warned of a changing national narrative that could erode civic feeling and create a negative fantasy of the nation's past.[11]

By the 1990s, many academic societies, teachers' organizations, and state panels argued for increased attention to minority groups, race, class, and gender. "Multiple perspectives" were deemed essential, and repudiating Eurocentrism touted as a way to root out pervasive cultural bias.

Throughout the 1980s, leading historians cautioned against the tribalism at the core of multiculturalism. Historian Arthur Schlesinger joined them in his 1991 book, *The Disuniting of America.*[12]

In deriding the so-called triumphalism of the old American history, advocates for multiculturalism offered a new paradigm that went beyond inclusion to redraw the national record. Core topics — the establishment of republican government and federalism, the development of a fruitful national economy, the extension of voting rights and education to immigrants, blacks, and women — were deemphasized.

By the mid-1990s, a once seemingly benign movement now conceptualized diversity in narrow terms; moreover, it merged with "critical pedagogy" to cultivate negative attitudes toward white Americans and traditional history curricula.

Americans once presented as heroic pioneers, religious dissenters, and immigrants fleeing Old World poverty became figures in a story of European invasion, slaveholding, slaughter of native peoples, religious intolerance, and other injustices.

Influenced by Howard Zinn's *A People's History of the United States* and James W. Loewen's *Lies My Teacher Told Me*, many teachers told a new and downbeat story of the nation's past.[13]

To judge by the NAEP and other tests, the multiple perspectives approach has failed to improve student knowledge of U.S. history. But it has left many students alienated from our political principles and from the basic act of civic participation — voting.

Rise of world history

As Western civilization was compressed and reshaped, students' gaze was directed away from the West and Atlantic civilization. Figures such as Julius Caesar, Marcus Aurelius, Copernicus, Magellan, Louis XIV, Mozart, Napoleon, and Darwin — who played key roles in shaping Western European and U.S. history — have been diminished or lost.

While critical of Christianity, European expansion, capitalism, and industrial civilization, revised world history instructional materials are generous or lyrical about African, Arab, and Asian achievements. They are crafted to fit partisan views of global wealth and poverty. Facing pressure from groups demanding inclusion or favorable treatment, education officials and textbook editors continually rewrite state curriculum frameworks and instructional materials.[14]

How Changes to the History Curriculum Occurred

The push for higher standards originated in efforts to overcome the academic mediocrity described in *A Nation at Risk*. California developed new state history standards in 1986, but the 1990s saw pressure from academic organizations and single-issue interest groups that undercut those efforts.

Mandated social content in instructional materials

Multicultural-friendly state departments of education such as New York's deliberately encased the tenets of multiculturalism in textbook oversight and state standards.[15]

New York said its 1989 social studies curriculum had valued "Anglo-Saxon norms" at the expense of other ethnic standards, exhibited "deep-seated pathologies of racial hatred," and constrained "the critical thinking of youth because of its hidden assumptions of white supremacy and white nationalism."

By 2000, California had created a powerful content armature to which curriculum developers, textbook editors, and district-level supervisors still adhere. Special concerns included race, class, gender, age, ability, sexuality, religion, and the environment. California prohibited instructional materials that contain "any matter reflecting adversely upon persons on the basis of race or ethnicity, gender, religion, disability, nationality, or sexual orientation...."[16]

California's 2011 Fair, Accurate, Inclusive, and Respectful (FAIR) Education Act, requires textbook publishers to draw attention to lesbian, gay, bisexual, and transgender figures at all grade levels.

Such legislation amounts to legislative malpractice, as it recognizes people not for their achievements or significance but for ascriptive conditions such as race, gender, and sexual orientation.

California's legislature is responsible for another act of malpractice. In March 2010, the Texas State Board of Education voted to adopt revisions to their social studies standards that were objectionable to progressives.

In response, the California legislature passed a law—the Yee Bill—that presumed changes to the Texas curriculum would have a national impact on textbook content and were driven by an inappropriate ideological desire to influence academic standards.

But who gets to decide what constitutes widely accepted historical teachings? Any effort to compose national history standards faces cultural agitators on the left and the right and must address partisan historiography, as well as how the media portrays such controversies.

The Texas curriculum was much less radical than the media claimed. California's effort to portray the Texas curriculum as radical and sinister heralds a future driven toward identity politics and away from academic soundness.[17]

The baleful influence of identity politics

Since 1994, state standards, diversity guidelines, and criteria for social content have helped persuade curriculum overseers that multiple perspectives and group identity are central to social studies programs.

Meanwhile, the economics of textbook publishing has meant increased disintegration of meaningful ways to monitor and shape curricula. Teachers have little choice in instructional materials offered by three major school publishers — McGraw-Hill, Pearson, and Houghton Mifflin Harcourt.

Meanwhile, decades of directives from partisans on the left and right have made identity politics foundational in curriculum development. Efforts to protect or add still more perspectives to those already crowding state guidelines, standards, and curriculum materials seem likely to continue.

Issues in Curriculum Placement, Teacher Qualifications, and Pedagogy

Early U.S. history and Western civilization are disappearing from many undergraduate and graduate programs, yet teachers are expected to teach complex political history at early grade levels, where in-depth understanding is not possible for most students. Teachers also often struggle with faulty curriculum placement.

Curriculum placement for history and U.S. government

In the 2006 version of the K–8 Arkansas social studies standards, for example, students study U.S. history, government, and citizenship, along with economics, environmental studies, and geography, in every grade. No grade offers a chronological survey of all U.S. history. The Founding appears at different grade levels.

Unfortunately, Arkansas' standards about the constitutional period appear in grade 6, when basic political principles may not be readily grasped. In many other states, the first coverage of the constitutional period is in grade 5. But most fifth graders do not easily grasp basic political principles and lack the background knowledge and vocabulary needed if they are to read seminal documents.

Traditionally, many students studied U.S. history and the Founding in grade 8, in part due to the theory of the "spiral curriculum" popular decades ago. It suggested that:

- Grade 5 cover from Columbus' discoveries in 1492 to the War of 1812

- Grade 8 review the American Revolution and then cover from the Founding to Reconstruction
- Grade 11 review the Founding and then cover from Reconstruction to the present

The problem is that when grade 8 includes the most intensive study of the Founding, schools do not offer a comprehensive history survey in grade 11. Thus, students don't learn much about advanced topics such as the Enlightenment, John Locke, Montesquieu, or *The Federalist Papers.*

Qualifications of U.S. history and government teachers

According to a 2006 brief from the National Center for Education Statistics, "Fewer than half (45 percent) of history students at the secondary level in 1999–2000 were taught by teachers who had a postsecondary major or minor in history.[18]

Most students are taught by a teacher certified in social studies. But by not making clear what a license in social studies means and by lumping all secondary teachers of history together, these statistics make the situation look far better than it is.[19]

In many rural schools, grade 8 teachers hold a middle school generalist or K–8 license. Their most recent coursework on the Founding may have been when they were in middle school.

What Massachusetts did in revising its licensing regulations and licensure tests for history and government teachers may be informative for other states. Until the early 2000s, most teachers of history were licensed as social studies and not history teachers. The 2000 revision of the state's licensure regulations:

- Abolished the K–8 license, the middle school generalist license, and the social studies license
- Made clear that prospective history teachers should focus their undergraduate coursework on four disciplines — history, political science, geography, and economics
- Created a political science/political philosophy license to attract students who major in political science to a career in teaching

Problematic teaching and learning approaches
History teachers and schools face obstacles in all grades:
- Time constraints include lunch breaks, recesses, health mandates, and nonacademic responsibilities
- Before junior high school, the basics of language and numbers push history and civics aside
- Compulsory mixed-ability classes mean fewer complex information texts can be used
- Principals try to meet performance floors in math and English but are rarely accountable for poor student performance in social studies

Activity-based learning
Social studies teaching suffers from project-based learning that schools of education favor and district and state curriculum directors promote, though little evidence supports its efficacy.[20]

Teachers are told that activity-based learning produces superior results while passive learning — lecture, reading, listening, taking notes, memorization, drill — torpedoes student interest and cooperation.

Activity-based learning makes special claims for success with children who are challenged by traditional models. When challenged, advocates of activity-based pedagogy deny that good communication derives from grammar and vocabulary or that gathering, sorting, and understanding require hard work.

Activity-based learning rejects the primacy of textual study of the Constitution, Bill of Rights, and amendments. Teachers are told that asking students to learn dates and geographic place names is unnecessary and destructive.[21]

Downplaying conceptual understanding
Many teachers are taught to dismiss objective knowledge and view history as "socially constructed." They learn that traditional Euro-American culture favors the dominant race, class, and gender.[22]

Workshops encourage Socratic interchange where teachers learn to be not a "sage on the stage" but a "guide on the side." However, when students bring no factual background or original insight to the subject, such exercises are sterile.

The increased emphasis on language arts and mathematics and other demands on teacher time mean the fundamentals that prepare students for a rich engagement with historical content are largely absent.

The result is to dismiss a view of history as a critical mass of ideas and knowledge necessary for students to gain a deep conceptual understanding of any historical event, figure, or movement.

Textbooks and Instructional Technology

Since 1979, textbook critics Frances FitzGerald, Paul Gagnon, Diane Ravitch, Gilbert T. Sewall, and others have commented unfavorably on history and social studies textbooks. They agree textbooks have lost sight of America's purpose, their narratives are thinner, and history is often distorted to suit interest groups.

The authority of textbooks in K–12 history and civics has faded. California and other large states do not have the content control they once had. Textbooks still hold a prominent place in classrooms, but one diminished over the last 20 years. But it is unclear what will replace them.

Usefulness of history textbooks

- Familiar, efficient, and relatively cheap, with questions to spark class discussions
- Useful foundation for teachers' lessons and written to reach a broad range of students
- Clear, organized sequences for teaching that few teachers can or will create on their own
- Prepackaged history and civics lessons work in the compressed time frames of K–8 classrooms

The challenge of digital materials

The digital revolution's claims to immediate relevance in social studies should be viewed with skepticism. Former Emory University English professor Mark Bauerlein and Oxford University neuroscientist Susan Greenfield have observed that the shift to electronic and digital materials seems to inhibit patient absorption of facts and concepts.[23]

Yet a growing role for digital media in social studies instruction is inevitable. It is easy to say, "Get rid of the dancing squirrels on the whiteboard screen teaching us how a bill becomes a law," but software developers know school districts want those distractions as a means of engaging students.

Today's flood of materials available online makes it hard to separate good instructional materials from bad ones.

The upside is a profusion of wonderful web-based materials, beginning with the National Endowment for the Humanities (NEH) Edsitement lessons for K–12, with substantive academic content.[24]

The downside is that ease of access may lead teachers to create lessons from shoddy or disreputable sources.

Moreover, the breakneck pace at which educational technology has injected itself into America's classrooms risks moving social studies classes closer to electronic infotainment. The pressure on traditional publishers to respond is intense, but their economics are ominous in a world where a digital textbook can be downloaded or projected, and a web-based curriculum is embedded with multimedia features and internet links.

The reality is that instructors want to access software and multimedia easily and frequently. Many will build social studies programs around prepackaged, big-screen learning modules, and will readily use nontraditional publishers. Discovery Education, for example, a Maryland-based cable media company with no background in textbook publishing, offers in-school audio-visual streaming programs in several states.[25]

An ongoing but lesser role for textbooks

Inertia and public pressure to keep books in classrooms

mean printed textbooks will not disappear soon. But their content — and that of digital materials — is problematic.

Teachers can be misled by graphic design and adornment. And with the profusion of nontraditional teaching materials, teachers may lack the time or judgment to determine what is good, better, or best.

Moreover, the variety of instructional media today has rendered the term textbook obsolete or misleading. Electronic resources such as Wikipedia have become the ruling authorities, even though they are not a substitute for sustained reading of the best textbooks and other works of history.

Efforts to Improve Civics and History

Once the anti-civics implications in history became clear, observant history educators, legislators, and jurists began to develop resources for teachers to counter these trends.

Traditional American history grant programs

Begun in 2002 and lasting for a decade, the so-called Byrd Grants were a paramount history and civics reform initiative. They supported three-year professional development programs to improve teachers' knowledge, understanding, and appreciation of American history and required that political principles and founding documents be explicitly addressed.[26]

However, a 2005 evaluation of the grants was inconclusive because evidence on effectiveness came mainly from teacher self-reports.[27] The consensus is that their quality was uneven and their impact on revitalizing classroom history was less than hoped.

Center for Civic Education

One of the first major initiatives was the Center for Civic Education in Calabasas, California. In 1987, the nonprofit organization developed its *We the People* program as an outgrowth of the Bicentennial Commission on the Constitution of the United States of America.

In 1994, the Center released the National Standards for

Civics and Government. These received widespread acclaim across the political spectrum and have been used to develop state standards.[28]

We the People focuses on American political traditions and institutions at the federal, state, and local levels, civic participation, and the rights and responsibilities of citizens. The program conducts local, state, and national student competitions on the Constitution and Bill of Rights.[29]

Some major public and private initiatives

The Lynde and Harry Bradley Foundation has funded civics education reform initiatives, beginning with The Bradley Commission on History in Schools in 1987. In 1988, the commission published *Building a History Curriculum: Guidelines for Teaching History in Schools*, offering themes and narratives for U.S. history, Western Civilization, and world history. The Commission later published a collection of essays titled *Historical Literacy.*[30]

The National Council for History Education (NCHE) was founded in 1990 as a successor to The Bradley Commission. It issued a newsletter, *History Matters*, and held many outstanding teacher in-service education programs and conferences over the years.

In 2008, the Bradley Foundation issued *E Pluribus Unum: The Bradley Project on America's National Identity*. It discusses the characteristics of American national identity, civic and transnational challenges, and the importance of civics education.

Independent textbook reviews

The American Federation of Teachers (AFT) and the Educational Excellence Network produced widely circulated critiques of history textbooks, working on the premise that publishers, states, and teachers would seek out better texts, lessons, and curricula.[31] Since 1989, the American Textbook Council has issued major reports and guidelines, including *History Textbooks: A Standard and Guide.*

Diane Ravitch's *The Language Police* and the 2004 Fordham Institute report *The Mad, Mad World of Textbook Adoption* explained how many state criteria distort the textbook market, entice extremist groups to hijack the curriculum, and result in mediocre instructional materials.

In spite of the efforts of alert educators and motivated philanthropists, not much progress has been made in addressing ignorance among students and teachers about the basic principles and institutions that shape their lives.

History of National and State History Standards

The push for higher U.S. history standards was sparked by the 1983 federal report *A Nation at Risk*. By the mid-1980s, a consensus for standards-based reform emerged among business leaders, policymakers, and educators. The best approach to weak K–12 achievement, they agreed, was "setting standards against which progress could be tracked, performance judged, and curricula, textbooks, and teacher training aligned." [32]

Background for first set of national standards

In September 1989, national standards and tests got a boost from Albert Shanker, president of the American Federation of Teachers, at a national education summit in Virginia. That year also saw the release of national standards by the National Council of Teachers of Mathematics (NCTM), which set a precedent for other professional organizations.

In 1991, President George H.W. Bush set forth his America 2000 plan, proposing national standards in five major subjects and voluntary national tests in grades 4, 8, and 12 so American students "… may be prepared for responsible citizenship, further learning, and productive employment in our modern economy."

America 2000 failed to win approval because it included vouchers and many legislators thought it threatened local control of curriculum and instruction.

In the meantime, encouraged by federal funding during the George H.W. Bush and Clinton administrations, along with other sources of funding, national standards were being developed by national organizations in English language arts and reading, the arts, science, history, geography, and civics.

In 1994, President Bill Clinton signed into law Goals 2000, which encouraged states to develop their own voluntary standards.

A controversy over national history standards

After President Clinton signed Goals 2000, the efforts of professional education organizations and discipline-based experts to develop national standards were slowing or coming to a halt. This lack of progress was largely because of the controversy over proposed United States history standards released in 1994.

Moved by California's successes in developing sound state standards in 1986, enthusiasm for national curriculum standards had grown. In 1994, a set of national standards were released. Sponsored by the National Endowment for the Humanities and produced by the University of California's Los Angeles Center for the Study of History in the Schools, these standards achieved their goal to "redistribute the nation's historical capital."[33]

While influential, these standards were accompanied by acrimonious debate and were repudiated 99–1 by the U.S. Senate in early 1995.

State of state history standards

In recent years, the AFT and the Thomas B. Fordham Institute have reviewed many sets of state standards in history or social studies. They should be applauded for undertaking the work of trying to figure out what criteria to use and how to apply them to typically incoherent and poorly written documents.

It is noteworthy that no other foundations or scholarly organizations at the postsecondary level undertook such reviews. Groups such as the Organization of American Historians (founded 1907), the American Historical Association (founded 1884), and the American Council of Learned Societies (founded 1917) apparently did not realize that reviewing state standards in their own discipline was as much their responsibility as the AFT's.

In the 1990s, the AFT issued *Making Standards Matter,* offering advice on writing them. They asked historian Paul Gagnon to review and rate the "civic core" in state history standards.

In 2003, Gagnon noted: "Not one of the 48 states (Iowa and Rhode Island allow local choice), nor the District of Columbia or Defense Department school system, wrote a document that had both a clear focus on civic/political education and was teachable in the limited time schools have to teach."[34]

The Fordham Institute did even more detailed evaluations of state standards, selecting scholars or other experts in a subject area to review and rate state standards in their area. Sheldon Stern, resident historian at the John F. Kennedy Library in Boston, reviewed state history standards for the Fordham Institute in 2003 and found U.S. history in poor shape in most of the documents. Sheldon and his son, Jeremy Stern, also an American historian, reviewed history standards again in 2011 and found little improvement.[35]

The Sterns found that the strongest standards:

- Offer coherent chronological overviews of historical content, rather than ahistorical themes organized in social studies strands
- Offer a clear sequence of content across grades, revisiting the content of early grades in later ones as students' cognitive abilities develop
- Identify real and important people and specific events and explain their significance
- Integrate political history with social and cultural history
- Recognize historical balance and context, such as the rise of both political liberty and the entrenchment of slavery in America and the growing conflict between these concepts
- Recognize America's European origins while also acknowledging the contributions of non-Western peoples
- Encourage comprehension of the past on its own terms, discouraging a presentism by which students judge the past by today's values, standards, and norms

- Are presented in clear, jargon-free language, with straight-forward internal organization

Conclusions and Recommendations

An examination of NAEP scores over the past two decades demonstrates civic and historical ignorance is high and rising. This ignorance poisons our politics, erodes civic culture, and effectively disenfranchises millions. Contemporary narratives in history affect how American students think about themselves, their country, and their relationship to the world.

Advancing American interests and democratic values at home and abroad requires clear sight as to what those interests and values are. If these interests and values are not known — or if they are taken for granted or scorned — the nation cannot easily endure, or it may do so in a way that conflicts with the ideals of the Founding and its civic principles.

Without civics or a shared past, the nation's citizens may conduct their international affairs in foolish or self-destructive ways or simply be unable to elect officials who make sensible laws and administer in the common interest while protecting freedom and liberty.

Where history is not neglected in K–12 education, it risks being drained of its narrative power. Demands for increased attention to world history leave students with an impressionistic and often inaccurate sense of the development of our nation and Western civilization; moves to correct previous distortion and omissions, however well-intentioned, risk substituting one air-brushed version of history for new, more inclusive air-brushed versions.

The results of a 2010 survey of Virginians by the Colonial Williamsburg Foundation and the Center for the Constitution at James Madison's Montpelier suggest the ultimate price to be paid for our lack of civic and historical knowledge. This survey found not merely a lack of knowledge about the United States Constitution but a creeping indifference, even disdain, for its principles.

- Only 27 percent of younger Virginians understand that the American constitutional system limits the power of government.
- A strong majority (68 percent) disagreed with the idea that the government is empowered to act for the common good.
- Nearly one in five of young Virginians (19 percent) thinks the rule of law is only a "somewhat important" constitutional principle.
- About 15 percent of Virginians think limited government and separation of church and state are only somewhat important constitutional principles.

By contrast, older Virginians were much better informed and demonstrated greater faith in the system. It is tempting to see in these attitudes echoes of an era of schooling before history and civics were sidelined.

It is difficult to find reasons to be cheered or to expect a renaissance in history in our schools. As a discipline, history has been stubbornly polite about its marginalization. Squeezed from the curriculum, viewed as secondary to reading, writing and STEM subjects, or reduced to a means of celebrating diversity, history has been abused, neglected, or hijacked across K–12 education. It remains largely absent from accountability measures.

The easiest response would be to demand national standards and testing in history. But there is little reason to expect these impulses to be fruitful. Rather than another stillborn attempt at history standards-making, we recommend states:

- **Adopt one of the highly rated sets of state standards in history and social science,** such as those previously used in South Carolina, California, Massachusetts, Alabama, Indiana, Washington, D.C., or New York. State legislatures, governors, and state boards of education should pass legislation or vote to develop, adopt, and implement content-rich U.S. history standards that describe our form of government, its philosophical and historical antecedents, and our nation's history.

- **Use the U.S. Citizenship Test at the end of grade 11** as a requirement for graduation from a public high school, admission to a public college, and eligibility for a Pell Grant or other public funds. A study by Xavier University noted that while 97.5 percent of naturalized citizens pass this most basic test of civic knowledge, only two out of three native-born Americans can do the same.

- **States might also consider administering the U.S. Citizenship Test to prospective teachers** to establish a baseline expectation that our schools should ensure students reach voting age with the same basic knowledge of history and civics we demand of our newest citizens.

A compelling case can be made that history and civics content has been systematically watered down without an attendant sense of widespread urgency or even a grasp of the effect of this on the nation's civic health and well-being. Former Secretary of Education Arne Duncan often described education reform as "the civil rights issue of our time."

When one considers the strong correlation between educational attainment and voting participation, this observation remains more relevant than ever. A sound, basic education can and should promote national identity, unity, and loyalty without indoctrination.

Cultivating understanding of and pride in America's history and ideals is an appropriate end of public education that in no way conflicts with the goal of creating independent, free-thinking citizens in a pluralistic society.

We become citizens by birth, but Americans by choice. Absent ties of blood and soil, a shared narrative and a set of common ideals is all that we have to unite us. It is all we have ever had. This alone cements history's demand on the curriculum and the attention of educational policymakers.

CHAPTER 2

The Rise and Fall of the Study of American History in Massachusetts

By Dr. Anders Lewis and Dr. Sandra Stotsky

Across Massachusetts public schools, history teachers believe that the study of U.S. history is in jeopardy.[36] To judge from recent national tests, students are graduating from high school with little understanding of our nation's history, founding principles, major institutions, and the figures and events that have shaped who we are as a people.

This is surprising in the Bay State because of the central role Massachusetts has played in U.S. history. The Puritans, who came to Massachusetts in the 1600s, created enduring forms of self-government and laid the foundations for public education. Massachusetts politicians, intellectuals, and writers — including John Adams, Ralph Waldo Emerson, and Horace Mann — have shaped American intellectual life and American politics. Many presidents — John Adams, John Quincy Adams, Calvin Coolidge, and John F. Kennedy — had roots in the Commonwealth.

Massachusetts has the ingredients necessary to promote the study of U.S. history, including a strong set of history standards and a commendable state assessment system. Despite these advantages, however, it is not clear whether Massachusetts students have even a basic grasp of our major political institutions, procedures, and principles by the time they graduate.

There was much progress in the early 2000s, when the Massachusetts Board of Elementary and Secondary Education adopted a new set of history standards (2002) and mandated passing a U.S. history test as a high school graduation requirement (2006).

But the board reversed course in 2009 by postponing such a test, sending a message that Massachusetts schools do not need to be held accountable for ensuring that graduates know the essentials of American history.

The consequences of that ignorance bode ill. A nation that does not know its past will not be prepared to make the informed decisions needed for the future.

This chapter:

- Explores the historical illiteracy of our students at a national level and suggests how to improve the teaching of history and social sciences
- Describes how the 1993 Massachusetts Education Reform Act and subsequent frameworks sought to improve the study of history and social sciences
- Recommends Massachusetts reinstate a grade 10 U.S. history test and make passing that test a requirement for graduating from any public high school

The Founders' Vision for History Education

The condition of history education in Massachusetts today would surprise our Founders. They knew that the preservation of our republic depended on an understanding of the history of the Puritans, the reasons for the American Revolution, and the causes of the War of 1812.

"History," Thomas Jefferson wrote, "by apprizing [students] of the past, will enable them to judge of the future; it will avail them of the experience of other times and other nations; it will qualify them as judges of the actions and designs of men."[37]

Benjamin Franklin knew that in a world of monarchs and despots, a republic was a fragile experiment in self-government. In

1787, when the Constitutional Convention ended, a woman asked Franklin: "Well, Doctor, what have we got, a republic or a monarchy?" Franklin responded: "A republic, if you can keep it."[38]

The Founders knew the American experiment in democracy would depend on the virtue, knowledge, and active participation of informed citizens. The people held what George Washington called the "sacred fire of liberty."

Horace Mann, secretary of the state's Board of Education in the mid-nineteenth century, believed public schools gave opportunity to all.

"Education then, beyond all other devices of human origin," Mann wrote, "is the great equalizer of the conditions of men, the balance-wheel of the social machinery."[39]

In an 1841 essay, Ralph Waldo Emerson declared that "man is explicable by nothing less than all his history. There is a relation between the hours of our life and the centuries of time."[40]

And in 1838, a young Abraham Lincoln pondered what would happen to a nation that forgets its history. He recalled the legacies of the Revolution.

"Those histories are gone," Lincoln said. "They were a fortress of strength; but what invading foemen could never do, the silent artillery of time has done — the leveling of its walls."

Lincoln's concern that the "silent artillery of time" would erase memories of the past need not have happened in any state. But it has. To judge by scores on the National Assessment of Educational Progress (NAEP), students in every state graduate from high school with little knowledge of our nation's past, founding principles, and institutions.

In Massachusetts, historical illiteracy has happened despite highly rated history and social science standards. Much of the blame rests with a 2009 decision by state education authorities to suspend plans for a U.S. history and civics test. Since then, public schools have not been held accountable for teaching to the state's K–12 standards for history, geography, economics, and civics.

To be sure, high school students in Massachusetts study history. But without accountability, there is no assurance they learn much about the U.S. Constitution, Bill of Rights, federalism, the three branches of government, and other topics central to understanding our republic and citizenship.

American Students' Lack of Historical Knowledge

Historical illiteracy among the nation's high school students has been discussed for a generation. It has been documented by NAEP history test results from 1986 to the present. Scores among students in grades 4, 8, and 12 in every state, including Massachusetts, have been consistently low.

As detailed in chapter 1, the 1986 NAEP results revealed huge gaps in students' knowledge of fundamental aspects of American history.

"Many [students]," as one study commented at the time, "lack a clear understanding of the fundamental document that defines the organization and powers of the federal government, as well as the rights and liberties of citizens."[41]

A decade later, in 1995, NAEP tests were still worse. More than 80 percent of students in grades 4, 8, and 12 failed to demonstrate knowledge of American history at the Proficient level defined as demonstrating "solid academic performance."[42]

Throughout the 1990s, graduating seniors headed to college or the workforce with minimal understanding of their nation's past.

"More than half of America's high school seniors," the *New York Times* wrote, "do not know basic facts about American history…"[43] On the 2010 test, a stunning 98 percent of graduating seniors could not explain the importance of *Brown v. Board of Education*.[44]

Causes of the Lack of Historical Knowledge
Distractions in contemporary life

Some scholars suggest that the root of the problem is contemporary culture.[45] In his book *The Dumbest Generation*, Mark Bauerlein argued that modern technologies—the internet, Facebook, smartphones, email, and instant messaging—stupefy youth.

"Yes," Bauerlein wrote, "young Americans are energetic, ambitious, enterprising, and good, but their talents and interests and money thrust them not into books and ideas and history and civics, but into a whole other realm and other consciousness… the rising generation is camped in the desert, passing stories, pictures, tunes, and texts back and forth, living off the thrill of peer attention. Meanwhile, their intellects refuse the culture and civic inheritance that has made us what we are up to now."[46]

In 2010, according to a Kaiser Family Foundation study, teenagers spent over 53 hours per week on electronic entertainment.[47]

Focus on pedagogy in schools of education

Others argue the problem originates in schools of education. Essays in a 2003 collection titled *Where Did Social Studies Go Wrong?* point to a lack of substantive professional training. Rather than stressing the knowledge teachers should help students acquire, schools of education have teachers spend inordinate amounts of time in professional development programs that fail to link pedagogy to content.

"We need," political scientist J. Martin Rochester argues, "teachers who have not only read books on teaching about slavery and the Holocaust but have also read books on slavery and the Holocaust. Process is not a substitute for content."[48]

That many history teachers lack adequate historical knowledge today is suggested by the errors that more than 20 Massachusetts teachers incorporated into proposed lesson plans after a week-long workshop on Islamic culture and history.[49]

Dominance of social studies

A major reason for the declining study of U.S. history was the development of social studies, which beginning in the 1920s sought a K–12 curriculum encompassing sociology, anthropology, psychology, economics, geography, and U.S. government or civics — leaving only the high school years for concentrated study of U.S. and world history.

Lack of a professional organization

K–12 history and civics teachers lack the support and visibility a national organization could give them. The K–12 curriculum cannot provide adequate time for serious coursework in all areas but might do much better with U.S. history and civics if there were a national advocate.

Ideology in the academic world

Many scholars believe anti-Western and anti-American attitudes have impacted teachers' academic coursework and are prevalent at schools of education. Since the 1960s, many college programs have become forums for advocacy or identity politics rather than scholarship.[50]

In *Save the World on Your Own Time*, Stanley Fish urged college professors to introduce "students to bodies of knowledge and traditions of inquiry that had not previously been part of their experience" and "equip those same students with the analytical skills — of argument, statistical modeling, laboratory procedure — that will enable them to move confidently within those traditions and to engage in independent research after a course is over."[51]

Reform at the National Level

The problems with the study of U.S. history have long been visible to political leaders and education reformers. In 1983, the National Commission on Excellence in Education issued *A Nation at Risk,* a ringing call for broad national education reform.

The report noted that "in many schools, the time spent learning how to cook and drive counts as much toward a high school diploma as the time spent studying mathematics, English, chemistry, U.S. history, or biology."[52]

Leading historians soon added urgent calls for reform. A 1987 report by the Bradley Commission on History in the Schools insisted that history "answers not only the what, the when, the where, and the who about the course of human experience on our planet but, of more importance, the why."[53]

But government reform got off to a politicized start. In his 1990 State of the Union, President George H.W. Bush declared that by 2000 "American students will leave grades 4, 8, and 12 having demonstrated competency in challenging subject matter including English, mathematics, science, and geography; and every school will ensure that all students learn to use their minds well, so they may be prepared for responsible citizenship, further learning, and productive employment in our modern economy."[54]

A year later, his America 2000 plan was touted as a "catalyst for change." Secretary of Education Lamar Alexander called it "a new voyage in the American experience."[55]

That voyage did not last long. The America 2000 document, produced under the direction of historian Gary Nash at the National Center for History in the Schools at the University of California in Los Angeles, was charged with bias. Critics said it emphasized negative aspects of history such as the Ku Klux Klan, McCarthyism, and slavery.[56] The positive was excluded or minimized. The names of Thomas Edison and Daniel Webster were absent. Even the U.S. Constitution was not among a list of 31 core national standards.

These ideologically driven standards were rejected by the U.S. Senate, 99–1. When the No Child Left Behind legislation was voted on in 2001, neither Congress nor President George W. Bush sought to make history a priority.

A Glimmer of Hope: Education Reform in Massachusetts

While national standards efforts foundered, Massachusetts forged ahead. The 1993 Massachusetts Education Reform Act (MERA) mandated state standards and assessments in all core subjects, "formulated so as to set high expectations of student performance and to provide clear and specific examples that embody and reflect these high expectations…"[57]

The MERA mandated that U.S. history standards "shall provide for instruction in at least the major principles of the Declaration of Independence, the United States Constitution, and *The Federalist Papers*."[58]

In 1997, the Massachusetts Board of Education, under the leadership of Boston University President John Silber, approved a history and social science curriculum framework.[59] Advocates of a substantive history education had reason for hope.

The 1997 curriculum framework

The Commonwealth's first curriculum framework for history and social science was strong, aimed at helping students understand our nation's constitutional foundation, fundamental political institutions, traditions, and ideals.

The 1997 framework called for the study of history every year, pre-K–12, with the integration of geography, economics, and government. Core topics included the study of Massachusetts town government, and the intellectual and religious heritage of Anglo-American colonials. Students were also expected to learn the roots of Revolutionary and constitutional thought from "Greco-Roman history, the Magna Carta, [the] evolution of Parliament, [the] Mayflower Compact, the English Revolution, colonial government, and ideas of the Enlightenment era."[60]

The framework did have faults, including a lack of grade-by-grade standards.

There were gaps in topics regarding the American Civil War, which omitted the 1854 Kansas-Nebraska Act that spurred formation of the Republican Party and the rise of Abraham Lincoln.

World War II topics included American isolationism and Axis aggression, but omitted the Battle of Midway, D-Day, and the atomic bombing of Japan. There was no mention of the influx of women into the workforce, the internment of Japanese Americans, or wartime efforts to end racial discrimination. And the frameworks were silent on the causes of the Cold War.

But the most serious problem with the 1997 document was its placement of world history, not U.S. history, in grade 10, undermining the hopes of those who sought to base graduation requirements on a thorough knowledge of our own nation's history.

The 2002 curriculum framework

Advocates of a strong U.S. history curriculum and assessment system used the process outlined in the MERA to update the 1997 frameworks. In 2000–2001, a state curriculum review panel conducted regional meetings, surveyed more than 1,000 history teachers statewide, and received more than 700 public comments.

Between 2001 and 2002, a network of educators and politicians, including a district superintendent, Harvard's Center for Middle Eastern Studies, Boston University's African Studies Center, and the Boston City Council, organized against the revised curriculum. Critics charged the new framework omitted key social sciences, did not encourage political activism, relied too heavily on rote teaching, and was too Eurocentric.[61]

Critics' efforts — including sending inaccurate information to the state's superintendents — did not stop the new framework, which was approved by the Board of Elementary and Secondary Education in October 2002 and distributed in August 2003.

The revised framework provided clear, grade-by-grade standards and gave schools the choice of placing a two-year U.S. history sequence into the high school curriculum, in grades 9–10 or 10–11.

The revised frameworks:

- Suggested overarching themes on the origins and development of democratic principles, individual freedoms, and democratic institutions
- Integrated skills in civics, geography, and economics with a historical narrative wherever chronology could be maintained
- Provided teachers with just one set of content standards to address at each grade level, together with related concepts and skills
- Offered a complete set of grade 12 standards for courses in economics and U.S. government

The rigor of the 2002 curriculum framework, compared to the 1997 version, created clear, measurable standards for a statewide history assessment.[62]

- As to the American Civil War, the revised version included the Missouri Compromise, Compromise of 1850, Kansas-Nebraska Act, South Carolina nullification crises, Wilmot Proviso, publication of *Uncle Tom's Cabin*, the Dred Scott decision, and the Lincoln-Douglas debates.

- On the Cold War, the revised version asked students to analyze the "differences between the Soviet and American political and economic systems" as well as "Soviet aggression in Eastern Europe." It included George Kennan's containment policy, the Truman Doctrine, the Marshall Plan, and NATO.

The framework's appendices listed the Declaration of Independence, U.S. Constitution, Bill of Rights, *Federalist 10*, Lincoln's Gettysburg Address, and superb history classics such as Bernard Bailyn's *The Ideological Origins of the American Revolution*; David Hackett Fischer's *Albion's Seed*; Richard Hofstadter's *Age of Reform*; James McPherson's *Battle Cry of Freedom*; and Gordon Wood's *The Radicalism of the American Revolution*.

The development of state tests based on the 2002 framework

The 2002 curriculum framework heartened advocates of history. As required, the state began developing a series of history and social science tests. And in 2003, the Fordham Institute declared the Massachusetts frameworks among the best in the nation, providing "a substantive model that many other states would do well to study."[63]

That same year, Diane Ravitch declared the Massachusetts and California history frameworks the nation's best. Without prescribing interpretations, she noted, each "builds a solid body of knowledge about history and provides guidance to teachers, students, assessment developers, and textbook writers."[64]

In October 2006, the Board of Elementary and Secondary Education mandated the passing of the high school U.S. history test as a high school graduation requirement, starting with the class of 2012. Chairman James Peyser stated that "our experience over the past six years has made clear that barely passing a 10th grade exam in two subjects [mathematics and English] is simply not good enough to prepare students for success in college or a successful career in the global marketplace."[65]

The following year, the department produced a 77-page report outlining plans for the history and social science tests.

Momentum was on the side of U.S. history. Amidst all the disturbing trends—low NAEP scores, declining civic participation and voting, and the reluctance of colleges and universities to require classes in U.S. history—Massachusetts was charting a more hopeful course.

A January 2007 poll found more than 95 percent of Massachusetts high schools required at least three years of history. And approximately 60 percent of schools had their ninth graders studying the first half American history and their 10th graders studying the second half, enabling these schools to administer the state U.S. history test at the end of grade 10.[66]

Momentum Lost

History's moment of opportunity did not last. On February 24, 2009, the Massachusetts Board of Elementary and Secondary Education, chaired by Maura Banta, voted to suspend for two years all state history and social science tests, as well as the history and social science graduation requirement.

Then-Commissioner of Education Mitchell Chester claimed to be "deeply committed to the teaching and learning of history and social science as part of a well-rounded curriculum." And board minutes indicated an intent "to establish a timeline for reinstating the history and social science requirement for the competency determination as expeditiously as possible."[67]

But for the next several years, neither Chester nor the board took any steps to do so.

In May 2011, the state board refused to commit to the test, claiming it was "contingent on the appropriation of funding necessary…"[68] In an October 2012 email to a coauthor of this chapter, a staff member of the Department of Education's Center for Curriculum and Instruction wrote that "there are no current plans to develop an assessment in History and Social Science for the Commonwealth."[69]

To advocates of history teaching, the state's decisions in 2009 and the following years were a stunning and discouraging about-face. As noted in newsletters of the Massachusetts Council for the Social Studies:

- The director of social studies in the Braintree Public Schools stated that "without sufficient knowledge in the various fields of history and the social studies our students will enter their adult lives and the world of work in the twenty-first century with a juvenile understanding of their roles…"[70]

- A former teacher at Bridgewater-Raynham High School who had lobbied to restore the test declared that its elimination crippled the ability of schools to fulfill their mission "to develop compassionate, informed, and active citizens."[71]

- A grade 8 teacher in Dracut pointed out that the state's inaction had led to apathy in many districts, which no longer see "the need to teach civics, geography, economics, and of course history."[72]

The president of the Massachusetts Council for the Social Studies declared, "that a basic education for any living and breathing American citizen would include learning about how the nation was founded, where the people came from, why they came here, and the significant events that have shaped our heritage and culture."[73]

In a letter to the department, he dismissed Commissioner Chester's arguments that financial concerns prohibited moving forward with the state history test. The state and local governments, he pointed out, spend over $10 billion a year on public education. The cost of instituting the state history test is $2.4 million.

Teachers are not alone in seeking a greater emphasis on U.S. history and civics education and a restoration of the state history test. A 2012 poll conducted by Pioneer Institute found 97 percent of teachers, 95 percent of parents, and 88 percent of legislators supported a stronger focus on our nation's founding and history.[74] And two-thirds of teachers and legislators supported reinstating the state test in U.S. history, with almost 70 percent of lawmakers saying the state could find funding to do so.[75]

Recommendations to Promote Teaching of U.S. History
Refocus the national debate on education

Any effort to refocus the debate must confront the national and state focus on math and reading. The 2001 No Child Left Behind Act (NCLB) required that any public school receiving federal funding had to test students in grades 3–8 annually in reading and math but not in any other subject. And the national focus on math and reading gained further momentum with adoption of the Common Core standards.

Although Common Core included content on America's founding documents, advocates of Common Core would not acknowledge that their standards were geared to reading and math, not history. In the absence of standards that explain what it is that students need to analyze, interpret, evaluate, and integrate, there may be little learning of actual history.

In Massachusetts, all the elements exist for a rigorous K–12 U.S. history and civics curriculum and test. The 2002 framework has won wide acceptance over the last two decades and needs only slight revisions.

The high school test should be reinstated with a clearer focus on our nation's founding, political institutions, and fundamental documents—akin to the U.S. Citizenship Test.

Teachers should focus on what is important to understanding our nation, not through rote memorization but through serious, reasoned analysis. For example, the 2002 framework asks students to "Describe the debate over the ratification of the Constitution between Federalists and Anti-Federalists and explain the key ideas contained in *The Federalist Papers* on federalism, factions, checks and balances, and the importance of an independent judiciary."

To meet that standard, teachers should discuss the goals and ideals of the Revolution, the shortcomings of the Articles of Confederation, issues at the Constitutional Convention, and debates between Federalists and Anti-Federalists. The capstone would be a reading of the most important of *The Federalist Papers.*

The Roman historian Livy once wrote: "… The study of history is the best medicine for a sick mind; for in history you have a record of the infinite variety of human experience plainly set out for all to see; and in that record you can find for yourself and your country both examples and warnings; fine things to take as models, base things, rotten through and through, to avoid."

Livy was right. Our Founders were right. And Massachusetts was on the right track when it insisted that students be required to demonstrate knowledge of U.S. history to graduate from high school.

Recommendations

- The Legislature should require the state Department of Elementary and Secondary Education (DESE) to suggest specific texts for grades 6–10 that would prepare students for reading a seminal text as juniors or seniors.[76] For example, Barbara Mitchell's *Father of the Constitution: A Story about James Madison*, Catherine Drinker Bowen's *Miracle at Philadelphia*, and de Crevecoeur's *Letters from an American Farmer* are excellent preparation for reading *Federalist 10*.

- The Legislature should require DESE to reinstate the high school U.S. history test as a requirement for graduation from any public high school in Massachusetts, with revisions to focus more clearly on basic principles and institutions, as well as on documents that reflect core American values.

CHAPTER 3

Imperiling the Republic:
The Fate of U.S. History Instruction Under Common Core

By Dr. Anders Lewis, Dr. Sandra Stotsky,
and Dr. Ralph Ketcham

Common Core and the Role of History in the American Experiment in Democracy

When asked to support a plan for public education in Kentucky in 1822, James Madison insisted it required intelligent, responsible, public-spirited citizens, with knowledge of "the globe we inhabit, the nations among which it is divided, and the characters and customs which divide them."[77]

The Founders assumed that understanding American history was essential in a Union that required citizens to live under laws "wholesome and necessary for the public good."

Madison, for example, noted that a people without "popular information, or the means of acquiring it, [was] but a Prologue to a Farce or a Tragedy."

Education, Madison believed, would place Americans of modest means on a level with the wealthy, promoting the interests of citizens and political leaders and the development of talents for the professions and occupations that would flourish in a free and self-governing society.

But what would constitute the proper content for the education of free and self-governing citizens?

Drawing on the legacy of Greece and Rome

Madison and fellow philosopher-historians John Adams and Thomas Jefferson began with their collegiate studies, where they learned Greek by reading Herodotus, Thucydides, Polybius, and Plutarch, and Latin by reading Livy, Sallust, Caesar, and Tacitus.

When Madison and Jefferson proposed works for a Library of the Continental Congress in 1783, they included many European historians and four authors that Jefferson declared at the root of American thinking at the time of the Declaration — Aristotle, Cicero, Sidney, and Locke.

The Virginians also recommended exploration accounts, tracts, laws, and treaties about the Americas since the Columbian discovery. They understood the importance of history.

Benjamin Franklin, growing up in Boston in 1715, had heard Increase Mather preach about the rumored death of "that wicked old Persecutor of God's People, Lewis XIV." When age 60 and moving toward the Declaration of Independence, Franklin remembered this sermon as his first recollection of commentary on public affairs.

How the ancients shaped the U.S. Constitution

Franklin's career was shaped by his knowledge of history and a moral perspective on it. Franklin noted in his autobiography that though he had had only two months of formal schooling, "from a child I was fond of Reading and all the little money that came into my Hands was ever laid out in Books."

From *Plutarch's Lives* Franklin learned ancient history and its concern for the commonweal and the public character of its leaders. He conveyed those values to the Constitutional Convention of 1787.

James Madison had acquired a knowledge of history in preparatory school and college that deepened his understanding of public affairs. He sought from his college friend in Philadelphia copies of Adam Ferguson's *An Essay on the History of Civil Society* and Joseph Priestley's *An Essay on the First Principles of Government*, books that would prepare him for the Virginia conventions and legislatures sure to come with independence.

Madison's library included books that Jefferson selected for him from the bookstalls of Paris, London, and Amsterdam. From these, he compiled a booklet, "Of Ancient and Modern Confederacies," that he used in 1787–1788 at the federal and Virginia conventions.

The Founders insisted that a knowledge of American history was essential in a Union "conceived in liberty and dedicated to the proposition that all men are created equal." All would have agreed on the shared obligation of all social agencies—government and non-government, public and private—to foster these qualities.

The Crisis in the Study of U.S. History

Today, nearly 250 years after the Declaration of Independence ignited the world's most remarkable experiment in representative democracy, the teaching of U.S. history is in serious trouble.

Although many Americans take their children to Gettysburg, read books by David McCullough, or watch the History Channel, history instruction in our schools is in disrepair. Madison might wonder whether we have reached the point of farce or tragedy—a nation with a democratic political system but a populace lacking in historical and civic knowledge.

At the elementary level, the National Council for the Social Studies (NCSS) has warned of a wholesale loss of instructional time resulting from the focus on mathematics and reading in the 2001 No Child Left Behind Act and in the Common Core State Standards.

"Abundant research bears out the sad reality that fewer and fewer young people, particularly students of color and students in poverty, are receiving a high-quality social studies education," the NCSS has noted.

Nationwide neglect of history instruction

The teaching and learning of civics and history is not a priority in our schools or among our nation's leaders. Most states do not require certification in U.S. government for government teachers.[78] The Center for Information and Research on Civic Learning and Engagement found that in 2001, only 34 states administered social studies assessments. By 2012–2013, the number was 21.[79]

Some leading Americans have voiced concern. In 2008, former U.S. Supreme Court Justice Sandra Day O'Connor and Rep. Lee Hamilton of Indiana wrote that a healthy democracy requires informed, knowledgeable citizens but "too many people today do not understand how our political system works."[80]

In a 2011 article, O'Connor and U.S. Secretary of Education Arne Duncan wrote that "Civic knowledge is not inherited through the gene pool. It is learned — at school and at the dinner table. And, too often, our schools are doing a poor job of transmitting civic knowledge."[81]

O'Connor and Duncan also pointed out that the crisis of historical and civics-based learning is most acute among African Americans and Hispanics. Statistics from the National Assessment of Education Progress (NAEP) confirm this.

On the 2010 NAEP U.S. history test, demonstrating a basic understanding of U.S. history content required achieving a score of 294. The average score for African Americans was 268. For Hispanic Americans it was 275. For white Americans it was 296.[82]

Such gaps in educational achievement demand attention, but state and national leaders seem to be looking the other way. NAEP administrators eliminated U.S. history and civics assessments for grades 4 and 12. Even Massachusetts, which has some of the nation's strongest K–12 history standards, suspended its history assessments in 2009.[83]

How did a nation that once believed the learning of history was fundamental to the success of democracy become a nation in which the evolution of democracy and of a republican form of government is minimized, ignored, left to chance, or politicized?

The History of History Education

Prior to the American Revolution, schools focused on religious instruction. The Puritans who came to Massachusetts in the 1600s believed reading was essential for understanding the Bible. Puritans established the nation's first public high school, Boston Latin School, in 1635. The next year, they established the first college, Harvard, to train lawyers and ministers. Puritans later required the establishment of locally supported elementary and grammar schools as towns became incorporated.

Although most colonists received little or no history education in the seventeenth and early eighteenth centuries, that changed with the coming of the American Revolution. The Founders insisted that only an educated citizenry could protect America's fragile experiment in freedom.

"If a nation expects to be ignorant and free, it expects what never was and never will be," Thomas Jefferson noted. One way forward, Noah Webster believed, was to banish British textbooks and use books written by Americans.

"Begin with the infant in his cradle," Webster wrote. "Let the first word he lisps be Washington."[84]

After the Revolution, more educators rallied around the ideas of our nation's Founders. In Massachusetts, Horace Mann urged the creation of common schools that would provide all children with educational opportunity. In 1852, Massachusetts became the first state to require all children to attend a school — private or public.

Still, the history that students learned was limited. Many students read from popular books such as *McGuffey's Eclectic Readers* that were light on history but emphasized moral tales.

By 1900, common schools existed across the nation, with enrollment and spending spurred by waves of immigration. There was widespread acknowledgment among educators that U.S. history merited a growing place in the curriculum. In 1899, the American Historical Association recommended four years of history at the high school level: ancient history in grade 9, medieval and modern Europe in grade 10, English history in grade 11, and American history and civics in grade 12.[85]

The rise of progressivism in education

That report was a moment of promise for history educators, but it did not last long. At the turn of the century a new group of "progressive" educators began an attack upon the teaching of rigorous academic history that continues to this day.

In 1913, a committee led by Thomas Jesse Jones issued a report, "Cardinal Principles of Secondary Education," that argued history was irrelevant for the vast majority of students, who would simply go to work in factories. Jones said schools should instead offer "social studies" classes to help children acquire the skills they would need in factories.[86]

That anti-intellectual sentiment became part of a report created by the National Education Association's (NEA) Commission on the Reorganization of Secondary Education. In 1918, the NEA said history was too arcane, a topic that the fragile minds of many American youngsters simply could not handle. Social studies should trump history.[87]

The head of the Stanford University Department of Education argued that "We should give up the exceedingly democratic idea that all are equal and that our society is devoid of classes. The employee tends to remain an employee; the wage earner tends to remain a wage earner…"[88]

Post-World War II Changes in History Education

The ideas of these progressives led many states and districts to eliminate history courses. But after World War II — with more students attending school— a few academics wondered whether we were on the verge of producing a large class of people who lacked the necessary knowledge to be self-governing citizens in a democratic society.[89]

Still, many educators continued to dismiss the importance of history. In 1951, A.H. Lauchner told a convention of high school principals that "We shall someday accept the thought that it is just as illogical to assume every boy must be able to read as it is that each one must be able to perform on a violin…"[90]

In a 1967 article, "Let's Abolish History," social studies educator Edgar Wesley declared teaching history is "confusing, unnecessary, frustrating, futile, pointless, and as illogical as to teach a course in the World Almanac, the dictionary, or the Encyclopedia."[91]

In the 1960s and 1970s, the anti-history forces gained allies. New Left, radical, and multicultural historians, commentators, and educators urged a move beyond Western triumphalism and American exceptionalism to focus more attention on American Indians, African Americans, Hispanics, and women. The new movement offered simplistic and polemical views of the past and urged teachers to be activists who sought to change students' views.

Howard Zinn, author of the popular *A People's History of the United States*, declared that it was his goal to "awaken a great consciousness of class conflict, racial injustice, sexual inequality, and national arrogance."[92]

Declining test scores reveal deficiencies in curriculum

Progressive educators believed that their ideas were in the best interests of students, but test results declined sharply in response. From 1963 to the late 1970s, SAT verbal scores dropped from an average of 478 to the 420s. Math scores dropped from an average of 502 in 1963, to 466 in 1980. Student knowledge of history and civics, as NAEP tests would soon demonstrate, was also minimal.

Most damaging, the theories of progressive and multicultural educators were clearly not working for low-income students who face an enormous education gap in all major subjects, including history.[93]

After the issuance of *A Nation at Risk* in 1983, many Americans were ready for change. A group of noted historians and educators created the Bradley Commission and called for radical changes at the elementary level — the replacement of a hazy social studies curriculum with a curriculum focused on actual historical content as well as biography, literature, and geography. At the secondary level, the Commission called for students to study four years of history, including world history, Western history, and U.S. history.

As detailed in chapters 1 and 2, national efforts to reform education fell victim to controversy and ideology. But several states developed their own rigorous history standards.

California's grade 11 standards on the civil rights movement, for example, required study of *Brown v. Board of Education*, understanding Martin Luther King Jr.'s "philosophical and religious dedication to nonviolence," and familiarity with Rosa Parks, school integration, the 1963 March on Washington, and the Selma to Montgomery marches in 1965. Books included *The Autobiography of Malcolm X* and Richard Wright's *Native Son*.[94]

The progressive assault on state frameworks

But progressive educators at schools of education continued to fight against serious academic history. Theodore Sizer, former dean of the Harvard Graduate School of Education, insisted that detailed state frameworks, no matter how scholarly, were attacks on intellectual freedom."[95]

Education writer Jonathan Kozol insisted that assessments based on the state standards smacked of memories of "another social order not so long ago that regimented all its children…to march with pedagogic uniformity, efficiency, and every competence one can conceive — except for independent will—right into Poland, Austria, and France, and World War II."[96]

Radical and multicultural historians insisted that state standards needed to be more reflective of recent scholarship on race, class, and gender.

In his 1995 book *Lies My Teacher Told Me*, James Loewen argued that "Black students consider American history as usually taught 'white' and assimilative, so they resist learning it. This explains why research shows a bigger differential between poor and rich students and white students, in history than in other school subjects." The same, Loewen argued, is true for girls.[97]

But by 1995, New Left, radical, and multicultural historians had been transforming the nation's history curricula for 30 years. Loewen's claims were both wrong and insulting, suggesting that people can comprehend only the history of their own race or gender and only when it is written by those of their own race or gender.

NCLB and Common Core leave history behind

Added to these forces was the passage in 2001 of the No Child Left Behind Act (NCLB), which required that all schools receiving public funding had to test students in mathematics and reading.[98] Once again, history was omitted. And as states adopted Common Core standards — again only for math and English — history was pushed to the side.

In 2000, it had appeared that conditions were right for serious reform to U.S. history and civics instruction nationwide. Nearly a quarter-century later, it is clear that devoted teachers and educators must once more rally for genuine change. Current trends make clear that the historical knowledge necessary for citizenship in this country is not sufficiently emphasized or valued. Madison's fears are becoming reality.

Changes in the Advanced Placement U.S. History Curriculum

The culmination of many of the recent trends that have shaped history education can be found in the College Board's curriculum for Advanced Placement U.S. History (APUSH).

The APUSH curriculum focuses heavily on the trendy issue of identity, asking students to "explain how various identities, cultures, and values have been preserved or changed in different contexts of U.S. history with special attention given to the formation of gender, class, racial, and ethnic identities."[99]

Putting current ideology ahead of history

The College Board appears to want a high school history curriculum that mirrors the ideological proclivities of much that passes for academic scholarship today.

For example, the board has nothing to say about Indian methods of warfare and captivity, including the use of ritualistic torture, but is relentless in castigating Europeans, particularly the English, as racist. It also notes the "strong belief in British racial and cultural superiority" and the "racial stereotyping and the development of strict racial categories among British colonists…"[100] Whatever else the British settlers brought to this country — including the critical idea of their rights as Englishmen — is missing.

Similarly, the College Board paints a dark picture of the Industrial Revolution, highlighting unions' struggles for control over wages and working conditions[101] but failing to note that most workers never joined unions and millions of immigrants to America embraced the Industrial Revolution and the increased standard of living it brought.

Political movements in the 1960s and 1970s led by Latinos and American Indians are said to be motivated by a concern for "social and economic equality and a redress of past injustices." Conservatives, on the other hand, "fearing juvenile delinquency, urban unrest, and challenges to the traditional family, increasingly promoted their own values and ideology."[102]

An incomplete and imbalanced view of modern U.S. history

The Board does not refer to the events of September 11, 2001, as terrorist attacks, and omits any mention of Al Qaeda or Osama bin Laden. It focuses on the "lengthy, controversial conflicts in Afghanistan and Iraq" and questions about civil liberties and human rights. These are worthy topics. However, without an understanding of Al Qaeda, bin Laden, their hatred of the U.S. and Israel, and their desire to kill as many innocent people as possible, students can hardly understand or discuss America's response to terrorism in any meaningful way.[103]

Clarity, balance, and depth are lacking in the APUSH curriculum. The result is a portrait of America as a dystopian society — riddled with racism, violence, hypocrisy, greed, imperialism, and injustice. Stories of national triumph, great feats of learning, and the legacies of America's great heroes are downplayed.

We next examine more closely how Common Core negatively impacts the teaching and learning of history.

How Common Core Threatens the Study of U.S. History

It sounds excessively dramatic to say that Common Core's English language arts (ELA) standards threaten the study of history. In this section we show why, in the words of a high school teacher, "if implemented as their authors intend, the Common Core will damage history education."[104]

How Common Core Came to Include Study of History

We first clarify how the study of history in K–12 got tangled up in Common Core's ELA standards.

The sad story begins with a document titled Common Core Standards for English Language Arts and Literacy in History/Social Studies, Science, and Technical Subjects.[105]

The backbone of Common Core is found in the standards for English Language Arts, which articulate core knowledge and skills. But Common Core also provides literacy standards for other subjects in grades 6–12, with the goal of preparing students for college and careers in multiple disciplines.

The standards allow teachers to use their expertise to meet specific challenges of reading, writing, speaking, listening, and language in their respective fields, but are meant to supplement content standards in those other subjects, not replace them. It is up to states to determine how to use what Common Core offers.

As indicated, Common Core's literacy standards are justified on the grounds that college readiness means being able to read, write, and speak in all subject areas — a reasonable expectation if the "all" doesn't mean every subject taught in college or a level of proficiency beyond the level of the coursework in the subjects taught in a typical high school.

The initial, September 2009 public draft of the ELA standards made the standards writers' vision clearer than the final version. That draft expected students in English classes to "demonstrate facility with the specific reading demands of texts drawn from different disciplines, including history, literature, science, and mathematics."

That original draft was the basis for entangling the study of history with what became the final version of Common Core's ELA document. But the attempt to make English teachers responsible for teaching high school students how to read history, science, and mathematics textbooks was soon relaxed. Critics offered a common-sense argument: English teachers could not possibly teach students how to read textbooks in disciplines they themselves are not expected to understand.

Nevertheless, Common Core's ELA standards still expect English teachers to spent about 50 percent of their reading instructional time — at every grade level — teaching "informational" texts.

What Are Common Core's Literacy Standards?

Common Core's literacy standards are clearly not academic, or content, standards, as the introduction to its ELA document promised. They are statements of different purposes for reading and writing in any subject. Here are three examples of standards for History/Social Studies in grades 11 and 12.

- **Integration of Knowledge and Ideas, CCSS.ELA-Literacy. RH.11–12.7**
  Integrate and evaluate multiple sources of information presented in diverse formats and media (e.g., visually, quantitatively, as well as in words) in order to address a question or solve a problem.

- **CCSS.ELA-Literacy.RH.11–12.8**
  Evaluate an author's premises, claims, and evidence by corroborating or challenging them with other information.

- **CCSS.ELA-Literacy.RH.11–12.9**
  Integrate information from diverse sources, both primary and secondary, into a coherent understanding of an idea or event, noting discrepancies among sources.

What is telling in the introduction to the overall Common Core standards is the expectation that subject teachers are to teach students how to read, write, and talk in their subjects, not the other way around. Teachers are not to draw on students' reading, writing, and speaking skills, i.e., their intellectual or thinking processes, to learn the content of their disciplines.

The introduction of Common Core in 2010 turned secondary school learning on its head with few or no objections from history, science, or mathematics teachers or their professional organizations. That is probably because most subject teachers did not know they were being required to teach reading and writing in a document ostensibly designated for English and reading teachers.

How Common Core Damages the K–12 History Curriculum

The underlying problem is revealed by the titles offered in an appendix to the Common Core. There, the document offers examples of the informational reading that history, English, science, and mathematics teachers could use to boost their students' reading and teach disciplinary reading and writing skills. The standards writers clearly do not understand the high school curriculum.

Inappropriate examples for informational reading

The standards writers apparently wanted to make teachers across the curriculum as responsible for teaching "literacy" as English teachers. At first, that sounds fair, even noble. But to judge from the sample titles they offer, students are expected to develop information literature without a coherent, sequential, and substantive curriculum in the topic of the informational text.[106]

While strong readers can do this, many weaker readers will end up deprived of class time that would be better spent immersed in the content of the specific course they are taking.

- English teachers in grades 9–10 may be puzzled by the listing of Patrick Henry's "Speech to the Second Virginia Convention," Margaret Chase Smith's "Remarks to the Senate in Support of a Declaration of Conscience," and George Washington's "Farewell Address." All three are nonliterary, political speeches.

- But history teachers in grades 9–10 may be even more puzzled by the examples offered to them, including E.H. Gombrich's *The Story of Art*, Mark Kurlansky's *Cod: A Biography of the Fish That Changed the World*, and Wendy Thompson's *The Illustrated Book of Great Composers*. It's hard to see any high school history teacher comfortably tackling excerpts from those books in the middle of a grade 9 or 10 world history or U.S. history course.

- The suggestions for history teachers in grades 11 and 12 are even more bizarre. Along with a suitable text—Tocqueville's *Democracy in America*—we find Julian Bell's *Mirror of the World: A New History of Art* and *FedViews*, issued in 2009 by the Federal Reserve Bank of San Francisco. These two titles clearly don't fit into any standard grade 11 U.S. history course or standard grade 12 U.S. government course.

Inappropriate literacy strategies—a nonhistorical approach to historical texts

Perhaps the most bizarre aspect of Common Core's approach to literary study is the supposed value of "cold" or "close" (non-contextualized) reading of historical documents like the Gettysburg Address. While the proponents of Common Core believe such an approach "levels the playing field," history teachers believe it contributes to historical illiteracy.

Before the advent of Common Core, no history or English teacher would approach the study of a seminal historical document by withholding initial information about its historical context, why it was created at that particular time, by whom, and for what purposes. Nor would they keep such information from being considered in interpreting a speech such as the Gettysburg Address.

As high school teacher Craig Thurtell states: "This approach also permits the allocation of historical texts to English teachers, most of whom are untrained in the study of history, and leads to history standards that neglect the distinctiveness of the discipline."[107]

Thurtell notes that the study of history requires specific concepts such as evidence, causation, contextualization, sourcing, and corroboration—largely distinct from those employed in literary analysis. While both ELA and history engage in closer reading of texts, they have different purposes. The object of the literary critic is the text or literary genre being studied. For the historian, the object is achieving a wider narrative of human history.

The Founders' View of Federalism

Federalism is an essential principle of American government and stands as the creative organizing concept that allows the fulfillment of the basic ideals of republicanism, liberty, and the public good. In this section, we explore how the Founders' views of federalism were shaped and formulated, and how their vision can continue to shape thinking about the public good—notably about public education.

As Jefferson explained in his first inaugural address, federalism meant "the support of the state governments in all their rights, as the most competent administrations for our domestic concerns and the safest bulwarks against anti-republican tendencies; [and] the preservation of the general government in its whole constitutional vigor, as the sheet anchor of our peace at home and safety abroad."

The terms confederation and federation were synonymous in the eighteenth century, meaning a coming together of sovereign states to cast votes as government units, without the direct involvement of the people. But the word came to have a new meaning, embodying the form of government proposed in the new Constitution, whose defenders called themselves Federalists.

Speaking for the Federalists, Madison explained that some

of the Constitution's features were conventionally "federal," such as the election and equality of the states in the Senate, and the explicit designation of some powers to the national government, while others were reserved to the states. On the other hand, some features were national in that they rested directly on the people, such as the election of members of the House of Representatives.

Furthermore, Madison explained, "the operation of the government on the people in their individual capacities in its ordinary and most essential proceedings" was a function of a national government, which he now designated as the federal government. Thus, he concluded, "the proposed Constitution…is in strictness [according to the conventional definitions] neither a national nor a federal Constitution, but a composite of both," now itself taken to define the word "federal."[108]

The word thus became part of the larger ideology of balance or separation of powers seen as essential to republicanism, liberty, and the public good.

Achieving a balanced federalism in the American founding

In the conception popularized by Montesquieu, Voltaire, and many English Whig theorists after the Glorious Revolution of 1688–1689 in England, the balance and separation of powers meant "the supreme legislative and the supreme executive…a perpetual check and balance to each other."[109]

In America, however, an all-powerful legislature akin to Parliament was seen as a danger. John Adams thought it would reflect "all the vices, follies, and frailties" of human nature, and "make arbitrary laws for its own interest."

Adams recommended instead a legislature of two houses, a separate executive with veto power over the laws, an independent judiciary with fixed salaries and tenure during good behavior, and a sharing of power between the national and state governments—a federalism requiring separation of powers within the governments of both states and nation.

The extensive size of the new American republic also required a division of powers between the center and the peripheries. Under the American idea of federalism, the people could convey to both state and national government such powers as they deemed proper, as well as withhold those deemed improper.

'Man himself the depository of the powers'

As Madison had explained to Washington as the Constitutional Convention was about to convene, the mixed nature of the new Constitution was entirely republican in that all of its powers were derived directly or indirectly from the people and thus remained faithful to "the fundamental principle of the [American] Revolution … to rest all our political experiments on the capacity of mankind for self-government."[110]

Jefferson offered his own understanding of federalism by contrasting the care for "the liberties and rights of man" contained in the U.S. Constitution with the Napoleonic era in Europe, where all power was concentrated in the autocrats of Russia or France.

"The secret," Jefferson explained, "will be found to be in the making [of man] himself the depository of the powers respecting himself," by trusting as few powers as possible to the higher, more oligarchical branches of government.[111]

Whatever the more technical and legal issues involved in the operation of the federal system — especially the division of power between the states and the federal government—the overriding intention was to have the voices of the people heard and responded to. That might be achieved through federal, state, or local governments, their administrative agencies, or quasi-public nongovernmental agencies.

Listening to the public—in government and education

In thinking through how any public question being handled in the vast bureaucracy of the federal system could be true to the basic philosophical premise of the system, the first concern must be full and earnest attention to the various voices, advocacies, critiques, and proposals coming from the public.

Nowhere is the need to adhere to that principle clearer or more vital than in public education, which for more than 150 years has served to unite Americans of all backgrounds through a shared understanding of our nation's origins, history, and foundational principles.

As Jefferson had explained in considering the "rapid importation of foreigners" into the United States after the American Revolution, newcomers destined to take part in American government should be imbued as soon as possible with the principles of the new American polity. Only then could they learn to "harmonize as much as possible in matters which they must of necessity transact together" with other citizens.

Seeking the public good through civil government

Jefferson supposed that a combination of federal law on immigration and state laws on education that were in effect a common core based on historical studies, would be the republican way to seek the public good in one critical area.

Jefferson's ideas illustrate how the civic core spelled out by historian Paul Gagnon in *Educating Democracy,* issued in 2003 by the Albert Shanker Institute,[112] could play an essential role in improving K–12 history and civics education throughout the United States.

"Civil government is the sole object of forming societies," Jefferson maintained. Thus, the understanding of the history of that formation must be at the center of the education, formal and informal, in common experience and bookish, of those who are, under the Constitution, to "transact together" the public business.

To fail to do this, Jefferson warned, was to risk the citizenry of the nation becoming "a heterogeneous, incoherent, distracted mass,"[113] rather than the public-spirited body good republican government required.

The federal system, built into the U.S. Constitution and state constitutions, as well as via the regular lawmaking and constitutional amendment processes, provides a unique and effective way to discuss and eventually fulfill this ideal.

Causes of Poor Reading in High School

We conclude this chapter by examining a critical shortcoming — how the Common Core undermines the most fundamental of all skills, reading.

Not only did the writers of the Common Core ELA standards profoundly misunderstand how reading in a history class differs from reading in a literature class, but they also misunderstood the causes of the educational problem they sought to remedy through Common Core.

The Core's standards were meant to identify and help high school graduates who need remedial coursework in reading and writing as college freshmen and the equally large number of students who fail to graduate from high school and go on to a postsecondary educational institution.

The architects of Common Core incorrectly assumed that the major cause of this educational problem is two-fold: First, English teachers have given low-achieving students too heavy a diet of literary works; second, teachers in other subjects have deliberately or unwittingly not taught students how to read complex texts.

High school teachers will readily acknowledge that low-performing students have not been assigned complex textbooks because, generally speaking, they can't read them and, in fact, don't read much of anything with academic content.

As a result, they have not acquired the content knowledge and the vocabulary needed for reading complex history textbooks. And this is despite and not because of the steady decline in vocabulary difficulty in secondary school textbooks over the past half-century and the efforts of science and history teachers from the elementary grades on to make their subjects as free of text as possible.

Educational publishers and teachers have made intensive and expensive efforts to develop materials that accommodate students who are not much interested in reading. These accommodations in K–8 have gotten low-performing students into high school, but they can't be made at the college level. College-level materials are written at an adult level, often by those who teach college courses.

Higher levels of writing are increasingly dependent on higher levels of reading. Students unwilling to read a lot do not advance very far as writers. The chief casualty of little reading is the general academic vocabulary needed for academic reading and writing. The accumulation of a large and usable discipline-specific vocabulary depends on graduated reading in a coherent sequence of courses (known as a curriculum) in that discipline.

The accumulation of a general academic vocabulary, however, depends on reading a lot of increasingly complex literary works with strong plots and characters that entice poor readers to make efforts to read them.

The reduction in literary study implicitly mandated by Common Core's ELA standards will lead to fewer opportunities for students to acquire the general academic vocabulary needed for serious historical nonfiction, the texts secondary history students should be reading.

Conclusion

We are left with an overarching question: Why were intelligent and educated people, including members of state boards of education, state commissioners of education, and governors, so eager to accept the opinions of standards writers who had no understanding of the K–12 curriculum in ELA and were not historians or experts in history education?

A further question is why intelligent and educated people did not read the appendices of the Common Core for themselves and ask how subject teachers could possibly give instruction in "literacy" in topics they themselves could not be expected to understand.

Self-government cannot survive without citizens who are willing to ask informed questions in public of educational policymakers—and demand answers.

Recommendations

There are several possible solutions to the problem Common Core's architects sought to solve — how to help poor readers in high school.

- Schools should establish secondary reading classes separate from English and other subject classes. Students who read little and cannot or won't read high school-level textbooks can be given further reading instruction in the secondary grades. That instruction can be provided by teachers with strong academic backgrounds, such as Teach for America volunteers, trained to teach reading skills in the context of the academic subjects students are taking.

- Schools should expand the notion of choice to include what other countries do to address the needs of adolescents who prefer to work with their hands rather than read and write. Alternative high school curricula starting in grade 9 have become increasingly popular and successful in Massachusetts. There are waiting lists for most of the regional vocational-technical high schools in the state. The trades they learn in grades 9–12 motivate them sufficiently so they now pass the tests in the basic high school subjects that all students are required to take for a high school diploma and over half now go on to some form of postsecondary education.

- The most important solution to the problem of poor reading—and an inadequate U.S. history curriculum—in high school is for state boards of education, governors, and state legislatures to disallow the use of the College Board's AP U.S. History curriculum in public high schools. Rather, they should require heterogeneous courses in U.S. history in which all students from all economic backgrounds, native born and immigrants alike, study together the common civic core spelled out in Paul Gagnon's *Educating Democracy*.

CHAPTER 4

Laboratories of Democracy: How States Get Excellent K–12 U.S. History Standards

By Dr. Anders Lewis and William Donovan

Introduction

The purpose of this chapter is to highlight states that have successfully written strong history standards and to suggest how other states can do the same.

We begin with a short history of the development of state history standards and then explore why teaching history is important and why we as a nation are falling short. We then offer an analysis of how six states — Massachusetts, New York, California, Indiana, South Carolina, and Alabama — developed strong K–12 history standards.

We conclude with seven recommendations that can help any state develop successful standards. They cover process, nonpartisanship, the importance of detail and clarity, the need to focus on academic content, the value of civics-based content, encouraging the reading of history, and the promotion of historical writing.

The History of State Standards

The landmark 1983 report *A Nation at Risk* called attention to the lack of time students spent learning core subjects, including history, and spurred creation of the Bradley Commission on History in the Schools. In 1987, that panel of leading scholars found that state history requirements were minimal and conflicting and were often trumped by content-light social studies classes. Samuel Gammon, executive director of the American Historical Association, declared at the time that "our citizens are in danger of becoming amnesiacs…"[114]

During the 1990s, well-intentioned efforts at national history standards stalled. One major effort, heavily influenced by New Left and radical historians, was soundly rejected by the U.S. Senate in 1995 by a vote of 99–1.

In 2001, the No Child Left Behind Act (NCLB) mandated schools that received public funding to test students in reading and math, but not in history. NCLB's authors, education scholar Chester Finn has argued, believed history was too politically divisive a subject for national standards, that schools had to focus on math and reading before anything else, and that—for subjects such as history—it was best to leave reform to the state level.[115]

In a 2011 review of state standards, the Fordham Institute, though discouraged by a lack of rigor in most states, noted that all states except Rhode Island had developed a set of history standards. And the Fordham report singled out six states for particular praise.[116]

Citizenship and Virtue
Why history is important and the dire state of history education today

Few Americans did more than John Adams to help secure American independence from Great Britain. As a delegate from Massachusetts to the Second Continental Congress, Adams was the most consistent and forceful voice for independence.

"Above all," historian David McCullough writes, it was "his sense of urgency and unrelenting drive" that "made the

Declaration of Independence happen when it did."[117]

Adams knew, however, that America would only last if its citizens were well educated—if they had the necessary knowledge and the moral character to preserve and defend a democratic nation.

"As long as knowledge and virtue are diffused generally among the body of a nation, it is impossible they should be enslaved," Adams wrote.

A core part of the diffusion of knowledge and virtue was support for learning literature and history, subjects to which John and Abigail Adams devoted their entire lives.

"Laws for the liberal education of youth," John Adams insisted, "are so extremely wise and useful that to a humane and generous mind, no expense would be thought extravagant."[118]

The example of the civil rights movement

American history is full of examples of individuals and groups who exercised such virtues to build a better and more democratic nation. One particularly important example is the civil rights movement, from which students can learn about the virtues necessary to sustain one of the most influential reform movements in American history.

Time and again, in the face of countless obstacles and dire threats, civil rights supporters refused to give in to despair. During his historic 1963 "I Have a Dream Speech," the Rev. Dr. Martin Luther King, Jr. told Americans that "We refuse to believe that there are insufficient funds in the great vaults of opportunity of this nation."[119]

Similarly, during his 1965 speech at the Alabama state capitol in Montgomery, given at the conclusion of the historic Selma to Montgomery march, King declared that justice was coming and that it would not be much longer. "I come to say to you this afternoon," King stated, that "however difficult the moment, however frustrating the hour, it will not be long, because truth pressed to earth will rise again."[120]

Civil rights advocates demonstrated a willingness to sacrifice their individual needs to the larger good of the nation. They refused to abandon the belief that America could and would do better. Their hard work led directly to passage of the 1964 Civil Rights Act, which prohibited segregation in public facilities, and the 1965 Voting Rights Act, which outlawed discriminatory voting requirements.

The central role of moral virtues in U.S. history

King's story and the larger story of the civil rights movement demonstrate how essential virtues — what Adams referred to as the "moral character of the people" — are necessary to sustain and improve our nation.

Today, few Americans dispute the importance of the civil rights movement. At the dedication of the Martin Luther King Jr. Memorial in Washington, D.C., President Barack Obama declared that King's story was "quintessentially American" because his story, and America's, is a "story of optimism and achievement and constant striving that is unique upon this Earth."

Indeed, all Americans should learn about King and the civil rights movement. Unfortunately, students are graduating from our nation's schools with minimal, if any, knowledge of either King or the larger movement he helped lead. American students consistently perform poorly on national history and civics tests. Ninety-eight percent of graduating seniors, to cite just one of many examples, are unable to explain the Supreme Court's 1954 *Brown v. Board of Education of Topeka* decision, which set the stage for the civil rights movement.[121]

"We are raising," historian David McCullough argued, "a generation of young Americans who are by-and-large historically illiterate."[122]

Core elements of a history curriculum reform

This need not be the case. Americans can choose a different path, one that returns us to the vision of an informed and educated citizenry that John and Abigail Adams thought so essential to the functioning of a democratic nation.

Reform will require:

- Commitment from schools, parents, state departments of education, legislators, and the federal government
- Strong, content-based professional development programs for teachers
- A renewed focus on hiring teachers with demonstrated academic knowledge
- Commitment of state resources to the development of mandated assessments
- A concerted effort by state legislators and education officials to write or revised K–12 history standards

Americans need not accept the existing state of affairs, and there is some cause for optimism. Several states, including the Adams' own state of Massachusetts, have written well-received standards that can serve as a starting point for the revival of history teaching and learning throughout the nation.

Here are six states that have made progress with history curriculum standards:

Massachusetts

In 2011, the Fordham Institute gave Massachusetts standards an A, calling them "a model of how history standards should be organized."[123] The standards were also applauded by Diane Ravitch, a New York University professor and nationally recognized education historian, as one of the two best sets of history and social science standards in the U.S.[124]

The 2003 standards are strong, reviewers declared, because they offer clear and exact guidelines for teachers, with a "substantive curriculum based on historical knowledge."[125] The standards were produced through an open process that reached out to history teachers across Massachusetts.

In 2000, staff at the Massachusetts Department of Education, led by Senior Associate Commissioner Sandra Stotsky and lead writer Anders Lewis,[126] started to gather input from teachers about the existing standards.

A history framework had been developed in 1997 in response to the Massachusetts Education Reform Act of 1993 but had limitations. It lacked specific grade-by-grade content standards and offered no list of important documents about which all students should learn.

The 1997 framework also called for world history to be taught in grade 10, whereas many educators felt that U.S. history should be taught then since it could then be tested through the grade 10 Massachusetts Comprehensive Assessment System (MCAS) assessments.

Stotsky, Lewis, and others held months of meetings and gathered feedback from more than 1,000 teachers statewide.

"It was a large process," Lewis said. "We reached out to local universities, professors, scholars, the Massachusetts Historical Society, to review the drafts. It took a tremendous amount of work. But we were happy to have so much feedback from so many people. In the end that's really the only way you can do it."[127]

The challenge included guarding against the politics of the day and partisan views of special interest groups.

"It's an inherently politically charged process," Lewis said. "When writing the standards themselves you have to try to be objective. You aren't taking sides; you just hope to write a clear standard."[128]

Lewis offers a hypothetical example of a written standard concerning the Vietnam War. A person on the political left might wish for a standard that says students should be able to identify the reasons why the Vietnam War should *never* have happened.

"That's a statement of opinion," Lewis said. "A better way is to say, 'Identify and describe the causes, course and consequences of the Vietnam War.' That is completely nonideological. Someone on the left, right or in between could say that that's fine."

One issue the committee faced concerned what history teachers wanted to teach in grades 3, 4 and 5 — U.S. history or a course of study that included more about India, China, and Africa. Teachers overwhelmingly favored U.S. history, largely because available readings were about U.S. history.

"In many cases progressive supervisors had been pushing down a multicultural philosophy on the teachers," Stotsky said. "But teachers said there wasn't anything for the kids to read. The kids weren't learning anything, and the teachers didn't have the experience."[129]

Stotsky instead proposed that grade 4 students study America's national parks and forests. Most teachers were thrilled.

"The people who were trying to impose multiculturalism were fit to be tied," she said. "They didn't want to study our national parks and forests."

The committee eventually stuck with the grade 4 proposal and devised standards that included more Chinese or Indian history as optional units.

"Teachers' concerns were less to do with the politics of the standards than the fact we were changing the framework just a few years after the 1997 framework," said Lewis. "Here was another adjustment made just after we had adjusted to the new framework. That was a fair concern. It was just a couple of years after, and schools and districts make adjustments, and it takes time."[130]

Another reason why teacher input was so desired is because Massachusetts students could eventually be required to pass a history MCAS test as part of the graduation requirement. That test would be based upon the standards.

"If the teachers are confused as to what a specific standard is, they will not feel the assessment system will work," said Lewis. "They won't know what they should be teaching. Standards need to be really specific."

The final draft was unanimously approved by the Massachusetts Board of Elementary and Secondary Education in October 2002. While the standards remain in place and have won praise nationwide, Massachusetts in 2009 suspended plans for a U.S. History MCAS test, undermining schools' accountability for teaching the fundamentals of U.S. History. To date, plans for such a test have not been revived at the state level.

New York

In 2012, New York State undertook a long overdue rewrite of its 1996 social studies framework to include significant historical events, such as the terrorist attacks of September 11, 2001, and the election of Barack Obama as the nation's first black president.

The K–12 document produced by the Social Studies Content Advisory Panel offered "a consistent set of expectations for what students should learn and be able to do."[131]

It was anchored in the New York State Common Core Standards for Literacy and Writing and the New York State Learning Standards for Social Sciences.[132]

The Fordham Institute gave the New York standards an A– and held that "New York's U.S. history standards are among the most substantively comprehensive and sophisticated in the country."[133]

Even as the content advisory panel set about its work, there was criticism about the state rolling out Common Core before new teaching materials were in place in schools.[134] The panel's work was also responsible for using an inclusive process that would make people aware of coming changes.

The panel included K–12 teachers from around the state, three college history professors, an Asian studies specialist from Queens, an economics professor from Syracuse, and people involved in state or national social studies councils.

While the panel could not change the elements that make up the framework or the sequence in which they were taught, they could gather input and shape the content itself.

"When we had a draft ready to go, we posted it on our website and sent a lot of eblasts out to professional organizations saying it was online for public commentary," said Steve Goldberg, a district social studies chairman in New Rochelle and chair of the revisions committee. "It was presented twice for public commentary for about four to six weeks each time."

Panel members were sensitive about any appearance of bias. For example, they recognized that many Native American groups in New York State would be scrutinizing how their heritage and history would be represented. And panel members note another potential controversy in world history, where teachers were required to teach the Holocaust, but could choose between teaching about the Ukrainian famine or the Armenian genocide.

"Not surprisingly, we got comments from the Armenians and the Ukrainians saying why are you optionalizing (those events) and requiring the Holocaust," said Goldberg. "Then you always get comments when you deal with the Irish famine because the British groups say, 'What famine?' Or the Turkish groups who say there was no genocide; they were siding with the Russians, and it was war."[135]

The committee filtered through more than 2,000 responses and decided to revise the grade 10 guidelines so that, in addition to the Holocaust, they would cover both the Ukrainian famine and the Armenian genocide.

While making sure to retain any sections mandated by state law, the panel pruned what members thought was a "content-dense framework that needed more latitude," according to Goldberg. For example, the study of Egypt was omitted from the grade 9 curriculum because it was felt Egyptian civilization had received sufficient focus in grade 6, and the panel realized schools have limited time to cover ancient civilizations. Similar decisions were made for other courses.[136]

Upon release, the revised framework was well received, according to Greg Ahlquist, a Webster, N.Y. social studies teacher, member of the content advisory panel, and New York State Teacher of the Year in 2013.[137]

Ahlquist credited the extensive opportunities for public comment, along with the presentation and rollout of the framework, for the positive reception. "There was a large feeling that we were being responsive to the field," he said.

The panel did alter the framework's design by replacing bullet points with major themes supported by smaller concepts and case studies designed for students to act upon.

For example, a unit on the ancient world titled "Expansion of Christianity, Islam, Confucianism, and Buddhism" used to offer students several questions to consider. The new framework offered a paragraph-length theme about the rise of belief systems and a concept about their purpose. It then asked students to "identify the place of origin, compare and contrast the core beliefs and practices, and explore the sacred texts and ethical codes" of seven such systems.[138]

In addition to reexamining social studies, the panel also looked at global history and the geography regent's exam, which was changed from a two-year exam in grades 9 and 10 to a single, comprehensive grade 10 exam.

The new framework also draws from the College, Career and Civic Life (C3) Framework, which was produced by the Council of Chief State School Officers in 2013 to enhance the rigor of K–12 social studies.[139] C3 includes the Inquiry Arc, an approach that makes the subject more challenging by developing questions and planning inquiries, evaluating sources and using evidence to communicate conclusions.[140]

The final document, called the New York State Common Core Social Studies Framework, was approved in April 2014.

California

In 2008, California's Instructional Quality Commission began a review of the state's History-Social Science Framework, originally drafted in 1988. A state budget crisis forced a halt to their work the next year, but their efforts were renewed in 2014.

The new version of California's curriculum framework, three times the size of the original, set expectations for what students should learn at each grade level, responding to legislation from the state assembly.

According to Kenneth McDonald, education programs consultant in the Curriculum Frameworks Unit of the California Department of Education, some of the bills were mandates, while others required that certain topics be included in the framework creating an instructional mandate for districts. Finally, there were "encourage" laws that function as suggestions.[141]

"The first thing was that there were a number of statutory changes," McDonald said about the revision process. "In 2011 the state passed a law mandating the contributions of LGBT individuals and the disabled to the history of California and the U.S. be included in the curriculum. So that is a mandate."

There were others.

Lawmakers have required the teaching of literacy, civics, voter education, the contributions of Filipino Americans in World War II, the farm labor movement, the contributions of LGBT individuals, the Obama presidency, and several genocides. They all needed to be written into the new framework.

"Course descriptions were entirely rewritten to incorporate new scholarship, and a lot of suggestions for teachers," McDonald said.

The new framework includes classroom examples at each grade level, links to the Common Core literacy standards, and links to California's English language development standards.

The framework and standards present content in a deliberate sequence "to develop thematic and conceptual understandings that span from the local to the global."[142]

In the early elementary years, for example, students learn about family and community structures, regional and geographic characteristics, and then people and institutions on a broader scale. In the upper elementary grades, history and related social sciences center on chronology and geography.[143]

The new framework calls for coordination between history-social science teachers and English language development specialists and a greater emphasis on civics than the earlier framework, with several appendices about service learning and civic education.

"If you pick one of our American history grade levels at random and start reading, you'll see stuff about voter drives and meeting with a congressman or going to a city council meeting, or students mobilizing to complete a beautification project in their community," McDonald said. "That's a very powerful force in California."

California's earlier framework was highly regarded, receiving an A– in 2011 from the Fordham Institute it for focusing "squarely on history (not on social studies theory or methodology), emphasizing context, comprehension, and chronological coherence."[144]

The framework was criticized by some conservatives:

- Williamson Evers, of Stanford University's Hoover Institution and former assistant secretary of education under President George W. Bush, questioned why "whole sections of the framework read as if they are pamphlets written by anti-globalization street protesters?"[145]
- The California Republican Party County Chairmen's Association called for changes, charging that the framework inaccurately describes capitalism as "inherently imperialist and colonialist" and makes no mention of the progressives' promotion of a centralized government.
- Stanley Kurtz, senior fellow at the Ethics and Public Policy Center in Washington, D.C., labeled it as a carnival of leftist bias and distortion[146] and claimed that conventional political history has been shoved aside by "race, ethnicity, and sexuality."[147]

The curriculum framework process began with the Department of Education conducting four focus groups of educators to get input on improvements to an existing framework. The Instructional Quality Commission recruited 20 people, at least half of whom were classroom teachers, to sit on a Curriculum Framework and Evaluation Criteria Committee. That group developed a draft framework.[148]

The draft framework was posted on the Department of Education's website for two 60-day public reviews and drew more than 11,000 emails. It received media coverage in Japan, Korea, India, and the Philippines. McDonald said 7,000 comments were received regarding grade 10 course language that stated, "comfort women were one of the greatest examples of sexual trafficking and slavery in the 20th Century."[149]

"It was inserted on behalf of the Korean-American community," McDonald said. "We got a lot of comments from them and… members of the Japanese-American community who were critical of those sentences. We made a few small edits, but they were kept."

The commission heard from more than 300 speakers at a forum to discuss whether the region that includes modern-day India, Pakistan, and Nepal should be referred to as India or South Asia, to represent the variety of cultures there and that India was not a nation-state until 1947.

"In most cases the commission recommended the use of the term "ancient India" but in some cases where the topic under discussion was broader "South Asia" was recommended," McDonald said.

Coverage of genocide was also controversial. An Armenian American member of the California Assembly led the passage of a law to encourage coverage of the Armenian genocide in the state's curriculum, and to reference other genocides like those in Cambodia, Rwanda, and Darfur. The language of the Armenian genocide was reworked, and more detail added, though the amount of coverage was debated. The other atrocities are mentioned, but to a lesser degree.

The final version of the revised curriculum was released in 2018.

Indiana

In 2013, Indiana undertook a review of its state social studies standards in the midst of a controversy over whether to adopt the Common Core standards. Three years earlier, Indiana had become one of the earliest states to adopt Common Core, with a planned implementation in 2014 and Common Core-linked tests in 2015.[150]

Instead, the state became a battleground between local control and federal intrusion in education. Opposition to Common Core was led by Indianapolis parents Erin Tuttle and Heather Crossin, who persuaded lawmakers that the national standards were less rigorous than the state's previous academic guidelines and should be repealed.[151]

In 2013, newly elected Gov. Mike Pence and state Superintendent Glenda Ritz joined Common Core opponents and conservative leaders in passing legislation making Indiana the first state to withdraw from Common Core. The new law directed the Indiana State Board of Education to create its own learning goals before July 1, 2014.[152]

"Indiana has taken an important step forward in developing academic standards that are written by Hoosiers, for Hoosiers, and are uncommonly high," Pence said.[153]

Indiana's decision to not use Common Core had very little impact on the social studies standards review, according to Bruce Blomberg, social studies specialist with the Indiana Department of Education.

"We convinced the state board that the social studies standards were good as is, so the board did not do any edits," he said.[154]

In fact, the revisions undertaken in 2013 were to history standards that the Fordham Institute had given an A– for "solid and substantive content, albeit with scattered errors and thematic departures from chronology."

Social studies review committees were created for every grade level, as well as a committee for high school courses that already had Indiana academic standards, such as those required for graduation.

Committee members included elementary and high school teachers, educators from Indiana State and Purdue universities, and private organizations, including the Indiana Historical Society, the Indiana Council for Education, the Children's Museum of Indianapolis, the Bureau of Jewish Education, the Indiana Council for Social Studies, the Indiana Council for Economic Education, and the Geography Educators Network of Indiana.

"We did a lot of wordsmithing and combining," Blomberg said. "We did do some adding of things pertaining to Indiana history that were glaring omissions. And we wanted to make our K–3 community approach more global than it was."[155]

The new Indiana history content included a reference to long-time Indiana resident Benjamin Harrison in grade 3 lessons on immigration, since Harrison was president when the federal immigration station on Ellis Island in New York Harbor was opened.

Blomberg said the 2007 standards were frequently accompanied by examples, which can sometimes carry so much weight that it becomes the only thing taught in a given class.

"We solved that problem by keeping examples in the lower grades because many of those teachers don't have a strong social studies background and the examples seem to be very helpful for them," Blomberg said. "But for grade 8 and above we took out the examples and created a resource document for the standards, which is kind of a teachers' edition for the standards."[156]

"Too many people think the standards are the curriculum," Blomberg said. "The standards are not the curriculum. The standards are the document from which the curriculum is created."[157]

South Carolina

When South Carolina revised its Social Studies Academic Standards in 2011, one goal was to create a design that simplified the standard for teachers, and another was to enhance the study of African American history. It succeeded in both.

When the Fordham Institute issued its "State of State History Standards 2011," South Carolina was the only state to receive a 10 out of 10 score and an A grade.[158]

The South Carolina Department of Education (SCDE) updates the state's social studies standards every six years. The 2011 revision, which aimed to simplify the standards and enhance the study of African American history, involved representatives of the state's 85 school districts, as well as the South Carolina Organization of Social Studies Supervisors.

The department also met with historical societies, the South Carolina Geographic Alliance, and the South Carolina Bar Association, and solicited districts and South Carolina colleges and universities for nominations to serve on review and writing committees.

Along with individual comments and suggestions, the review committee drew upon:[159]

- South Carolina Social Studies Academic Standards, published in 2005

- National standards, including:
  - The *National Curriculum Standards for Social Studies: A Framework for Teaching, Learning, and Assessment, 2010*
  - Common Core State Standards for English Language Arts 2010
  - Standards from California, Colorado, Minnesota, New York, North Carolina, Ohio, and Wisconsin
  - Resources on content and design of grade-level and high school standards

According to Lewis Huffman, retired education associate and the education department's coordinator for the standards reform effort, the committees were balanced geographically and by district size, represented multiple grades, and mixed veteran and newer teachers.[160]

In addition, the South Carolina Education Oversight Committee created three committees — representing businesses, special education teachers, and subject matter experts from around the country. Their input to the review committee helped shape recommendations for the writing committee.

"Social studies is not like math or science where you build process skills from year to year," Huffman said. "Social studies is based on factual information. Yet we were trying to get to the idea of not just remembering facts for facts sake but knowing them in order to build conceptual understanding."[161]

In addition to a descriptive theme for each standard in each grade, the format included an academic standard establishing the central expectation for student learning in each area. And the writing committee added "enduring understanding," which "identifies and briefly explains the main idea or central concept inherent in the standard that students should understand.[162]

The goal was to make the standards more manageable.

"Some teachers would look at the standards and think that they were so broad and big, and they couldn't wrap their arms around it," Huffman said. "They didn't know what they were supposed to teach out of them. So, we designed the enduring understanding to say 'This is the big takeaway. This is the big conceptual idea we want you to know.'" [163]

For example:

- The first "U.S. History and the Constitution" standard states students will demonstrate "an understanding of the conflicts between regional and national interest in the development of democracy in the United States."
- Next, the enduring understanding concept focuses on how democratic ideals that originated in England were transplanted to North America by English settlers and evolved "as a result of regional experiences."
- Finally come a series of indicators that provide teachers with additional guidance for ongoing assessment, outlining what knowledge and skills students must demonstrate. [164] In this example, one indicator asks students to summarize the characteristics "of each colonial region in the settlement and development of British North America."

The revision process took a year and included a support document for teachers, some of whom said they weren't able to get through all the content in the time available to them in an academic year. Teachers using the support document, Huffman said, saw their students' end-of-year test scores come in higher than most others.

While disagreements and controversies can often erupt when creating history standards, Huffman said that in South Carolina the open effort to create diversified committees helped keep those to a minimum.

Alabama

The theme of the 2010 Alabama Social Studies Course of Study is "responsible citizenship." The standards, updated from a 2004 version, expressed the view that through history education students become aware of the parts they play as responsible citizens.

The introduction to the document makes clear what

"historically informed" students should be able to do, including:
- Construct a personal connection to historical events
- Think critically and chronologically regarding major historical events
- Critique historical documents
- Engage in historical analysis and interpretation
- Conduct historical research
- Evaluate intricate connections throughout time
- Engage in decision making using historical knowledge and analysis[165]

Alabama's standards have been applauded for their thorough overview of American history, as well as their clear guidance for teachers and students.[166]

In creating the new standards, the 30-person Social Studies State Course of Study Committee identified four strands: history, economics, geography, and civics and government. All strands are included in every grade.

The content standard states what students should know and be able to do at the conclusion of a course or grade level. The first kindergarten standard, for example, states that students will "Sequence events using schedules, calendars, and timelines," and states that they should differentiate among broad categories of historical time."

The study committee tried to make the standards more detailed for teachers, and included suggestions for more current teaching methods, such as the use of technology in geography.

"Things have changed with the way kids learn geography with the introduction of technology," said Chasidy White, a middle school teacher and committee member. "The kids now have access to digital maps and geographical information systems. So, students were still expected to learn the same things but there were some added elements to keep up with the digital age."[167]

One grade 7 standard says students will describe the world in spatial terms using maps and other geographic representations, tools, and technologies such as Google Earth, GPS, satellites, and photography.

Members of the study committee were appointed by the Alabama State Board of Education and the governor. They included early childhood, intermediate school, middle school, high school, and college educators, along with business and professional people. The committee included the president of the Alabama Historical Society, a mortgage broker, and a parent.

The committee posted their draft for public comment, shared it with teachers statewide, and made changes when appropriate. For example, a proposal to move government and economics to grade 11 and have grade 12 be a modern world events class was rejected when teachers statewide opposed that move.

"That's when (students) were registering to vote or joining the military after graduation," White said. "They felt like government and economics needed to stay in the twelfth grade."[168]

White said members gathered with a nonpartisan point of view and worked cohesively as a committee.

"We had a great deal of discussion over every standard, and everyone offered their opinion," said White. "We weren't allowed to bring in outside material. It was just coming from our own knowledge background."

Recommendations

As this chapter has demonstrated, numerous states have written well-received standards. How can other states move forward and create new standards or, as Massachusetts did, revise existing standards in a way that promotes the teaching and learning of history?

Design an open, inclusive process

The states enjoying the most success with their curriculum frameworks are those that enabled the entire educational community to have a say. Most importantly, teachers need multiple opportunities throughout the standards design process to express their views. This could include surveys, regional meetings, and document review panels. Without such a broad effort to reach the teaching community, state efforts will be viewed skeptically, at best—yet another edict from bureaucrats with little knowledge of the day-to-day reality of life in the classroom.

Adopt a nonpartisan stance

It is not the place of states or history teachers to push their views about contested historical topics. Curriculum writers must craft standards that are fair and unbiased. Failure to do so, as the debate over the national history standards in the 1990s and the recent APUSH standards demonstrate, will result in failure. Almost every historical topic is subject to debate. Standards writers and education officials should acknowledge the debates but let teachers present numerous viewpoint and let students decide for themselves.

Make standards detailed and specific

State history tests, which we support, must be based on standards that leave no room for ambiguity. Teachers and students should not have to guess what will be on any test used as a graduation requirement. For example, asking students to identify the causes of the Civil War is an excellent start, but unless that standard identifies specific causes, such as the debate over the extension of slavery into Western territories, the test may well become little more than a guessing game.

Focus strongly on academic content

Education officials should craft standards focused on academic content. This requires they stand against fashionable current trends that are promoted as "twenty-first century thinking skills," "critical thinking," "problem solving," or "innovation." While these are important skills, they cannot be developed without a strong understanding of academic content. Students cannot think critically about the civil rights movement, for example, without strong knowledge of the economic, social, and political conditions that gave rise to it, including major figures such as Dr. King.

Incorporate civics-based content

The simplest way to promote the learning of material essential to understanding government and citizenship is to include historically appropriate references to fundamental topics such as the purpose and roles of the various branches of government or the rights and responsibilities of citizenship. Education officials should emphasize foundational documents such as the Declaration of Independence, the Constitution, the Bill of Rights; *The Federalist Papers*; the Seneca Falls Declaration of Sentiments and Resolutions; and speeches by Frederick Douglass, Abraham Lincoln, and Dr. King.

Require the reading of history

Districts should require students in grades 1–12 to read at least one history book or history-related biography annually to develop vocabulary and content knowledge. In the elementary grades, students can start with short biographies of inspirational Americans such as Abraham Lincoln and Jackie Robinson. In middle school, they can read short histories of the American Revolution or World War II. High school students can then start to read more complex history works aligned with the history and literature classes they are taking.

Promote historical writing

Teaching students to develop clearly written, thesis-driven papers with strong analysis and use of evidence cannot be done overnight or in any one year. Developing strong writing skills takes many years. To develop them, districts can require that students write a history essay each year — one of increasing complexity, length, and quantity of research.[169]

A final word of caution

Finally, a word of caution. As this chapter has sought to demonstrate, many states have exemplary existing standards. Educational leaders may feel the need to revise or completely rewrite standards to show teachers that they are interested in furthering the teaching and learning of history. But where existing standards are already highly rated, it is better for states to invest their time and resources in developing a statewide assessment system.[170]

Speaking in 2005, historian David McCullough remarked that "We have to get across the idea that we have to know who we were if we're to know who we are and where we're headed."[171]

Nearly 20 years later and in the midst of much political turmoil around the world, McCullough's words are more meaningful than ever. Today's high school graduates are confronted by a complex world where their choices have profound meaning. It is time to revive excellence in history standards nationwide.

CHAPTER 5

The Sacred Fire of Liberty

By Dr. E.D. Hirsch, Jr.

While public education—and how best to reform it—is often the subject of fierce debate, several organizations have for years striven to show that education does not have to be a partisan issue.

They include think tanks such as Pioneer Institute that focus strictly on educational research and policy recommendations, while standing apart from partisan politics. They include national nonprofits such as Bellwether Education—part think tank and part support organization—that are committed to dramatically improving educational outcomes for low-income youth and work directly with leading-edge ventures and leaders nationwide.

Even some clearly political organizations have joined the fight, including Democrats for Education Reform (DFER), a political action committee that supports teachers, higher educational quality, and public school choice, including charter schools.

This broad coalition in support of better education encompasses individuals whose ideas and writings transcend the usual partisan delineations of left vs. right and Democrat vs. Republican.

Two fundamental realizations

Many years of observation, research, and work in educational policy have led to the realization of two important truths.

These truths — and the ideas for reform that derive from them — have emerged from the work and ideas of many people, and there are many formulations and theories that seek to guide education reform.

Any reform agenda, however, is more likely to be effective if it can be expressed in a few simple, powerful words. "The Sacred Fire of Liberty" captures the mix of urgent action and cultural literacy that are essential guides to shepherding reform through systems that sometimes seem hopelessly complex and politicized.

The first truth may be difficult for many Americans to acknowledge, particularly those who understand that our traditions of public education have for many years helped build one of the freest and most economically powerful nations in the world.

But the evidence of recent decades is incontrovertible. Our schools—and we focus primarily on district public schools in this context—are dramatically underserving some students. In fact, some systems, including many of our nation's large urban school systems, are systematically failing the most vulnerable students.

The second truth, while no less challenging than the first, sounds a much more hopeful note: It doesn't have to be this way. A nation with the wealth, talent, and history of the United States can surely summon the will to reform its system of public education to strengthen democracy and freedom. Americans — who hail from every nation on Earth — can and should once more be models of educational excellence for the world.

Identifying the problems in curriculum and content

Years of research, along with a dose of serendipity, have helped identify the fundamental problem with American education. It can be summarized in two words — curriculum and content.

The fault with these two basic elements lies less with the debates over precisely what is taught in a given school and more with the shocking absence of both. It is the lack of rigorous curricular standards and meaningful content that have come to define too much of modern American education.

Through many years of debate and fitful attempts at reform, American educators, parents, and policymakers not only paid insufficient attention to curriculum and content, but the very idea of shared knowledge as holding value became suspect or considered to be a sideshow.

It's worth pausing on this point. Unfortunately, in our politically dysfunctional field of education, the idea of a core curriculum and shared knowledge is often seen as a right-wing or politically conservative idea.

For example, it surely didn't help that *Cultural Literacy: What Every American Needs to Know,* was published at about the same time as Allan Bloom's *Closing of the American Mind* and was consequently injected into the culture wars alongside it.

In addition to those who insist on seeing curricular reforms in a political light, there are those given to self-flattery about just how revolutionary the times we live in really are. They often view content as a mere feeder for learning. They deride content as fungible in what they consider a brave new technological world where anything labeled "new" or carrying the tag twenty-first-century skills — so-called critical thinking and problem-solving — is romanticized at the expense of content and knowledge.

The result is predictable: America's schools wind up paying insufficient attention to what it genuinely takes to transform teaching and learning.

A truth enduring through the ages: Content does matter

In their own defense, today's educators argue that when it comes to content and curriculum, it doesn't matter what kids read as long as they're reading something.

Is there a more vain or ahistorical sentiment in education? Never mind that it ignores that throughout the ages some content and ideas have been considered so important by societies that they have been written down and preserved, sometimes openly and sometime surreptitiously.

Christian monks, Muslim scholars, and Buddhist thinkers labored to preserve certain fundamental ideas about the nature of man, society, justice, and ways of living and experiencing human life.

But the idea that the content of children's reading doesn't matter is also at odds with what we know about how people learn and acquire domain knowledge and skills in the first place. The reality is that content is important to both reading and understanding. That's why the divides in this educational debate don't always fall along education's traditional fault lines.

The American Federation of Teachers, for instance, has long championed the centrality of clearly defined content for learning.

Championing content, then, is hardly to be considered conservative in any modern, political sense of that world. On the contrary, promoting and defending a rigorous, fact-based curriculum is better understood as a profoundly egalitarian stance.

Where the allegedly new meets the old

Throughout history, the elite classes in every society have always had the upper hand when it comes to new technologies and knowledge. What we today call twenty-first-century skills are really nothing other than advances in technology and new ways of engaging with the world.

From the days when the Phoenicians sailed the Mediterranean to the race to put humans on the Moon, advanced knowledge and skills have been the fundamental paths for human progress and advances in every age.

The challenge today is to recognize that democratizing the education that was once reserved for the elites is essential for increasing individual opportunity and the collective good. That is precisely why ideas grounded in the value of traditional learning — expressed in rigorous, content-rich curricula — are more timely than ever.

An ongoing national conversation about education

For the best part of a generation, our nation has been engaged in a national conversation about our schools. Often acrimonious and politically charged, that conversation has often focused on national standards.

In part because of the warnings sounded so insistently in the landmark 1983 report *A Nation at Risk,* the idea of greater commonality of subject matter across what remains a culturally, politically, and sociologically diverse nation has gained ground.

But the authors of *A Nation at Risk* did not prescribe a curriculum stripped of content. Rather, those who minimize content while romanticizing the value of supposedly novel twenty-first-century skills have dominated the conversation because of the seductive, albeit superficial, allure of their arguments.

Perhaps their greatest success was the adoption across many states of the Common Core State Standards Initiative. Launched in 1990, the Common Core is now the dominant framework for public education in 36 U.S. states.

Yet Common Core's triumph remains far from complete. In the more than 30 years since its launch, it has drawn significant criticism for what many consider its "lowest common denominator" approach to education. Rather than challenging the nation's students to aspire to meet the demands of a richer, fuller, and more intellectually challenging curriculum, Common Core has too often impoverished instruction.

While many educators and reformers have arrived at that conclusion through analysis of Common Core's content, the public at large has drawn its inferences largely through observation of the results of what has now been a generation-long experiment.

Recognizing the missteps of a generational experiment

Simply put, there is growing recognition of the abject poverty of civic and political discourse in these United States. As standardized test scores continued to plummet—and the U.S.'s standing relative to the rest of the world continued to slip—the response among too many in our elite and educator classes was to further relax standards, eliminate testing, and adopt attitudes that somehow, someway—perhaps through technology—all would be well.

America's students and their parents, however, have not been so easily deceived. They recognized that the ongoing decline in content and rigor in traditional K–12 public education is linked directly to rising dropout rates and declining graduation rates at the secondary level.

These parents have acted. Even as Common Core spread across the nation, so too has the movement toward school choice strengthened. The rise of charter schools, voucher programs, school choice, scholarships, and religious and homeschooling has given America's K–12 educational landscape a far more diverse profile than in years past.

Moreover, parents today understand that the deleterious consequences of this generational experiment are not limited to often woeful performance on standardized tests. They see each day a society that deemphasizes the study of history, ignores civics, and pushes aside the great ideas of the past. They understand that doing all this in the name of vague and largely unobtainable ideals of equity and equality puts at risk the qualities Americans need if they are to sustain and grow a strong republic.

It is precisely here that we witness how the thinning — or outright elimination — of curriculum and content has led to the loss of conversation, community, and civility as Americans progress into a new century, one whose daunting challenges demand those values as never before.

Why traditional educational values resonate today

As traditional values continue to resonate in the context of contemporary education debates, three points bear emphasis:

- **Shared knowledge is important as a tool of social equity**
  As we debate educational standards, who should go to college, and what the expectations for school performance should be, the idea of commonness — in the sense of sharing core knowledge widely — matters deeply. It is not undemocratic,

as some claim, to share the best educational traditions; rather, creating a shared and level playing field is the most democratic thing we can do.

- ## We must be willing to make hard choices in curriculum
  Too often, educators eschew hard choices by taking the easy path of opting for many or all topics when developing curriculum. The American Enterprise Institute's Rick Hess has written extensively about this, which he characterizes as "expansionist multiculturalism." In fact, a great curriculum requires choices and doesn't have to contain everything.

  Indeed, the traditional curricula grounded in Western Civilization—often derided by its critics as "celebrating dead white men"—is actually among the most substantively multicultural out there, teaching about the world in a rich way that fosters understanding.

  Meanwhile, the ostensibly more diverse curriculum pushed by advocates of multiculturalism often focuses on food, cultural trimmings, and trivia, while sacrificing in-depth study and understanding of cultural practices and differences.

- ## Reformers must not shy away from educational debates and fights
  The education debates in the U.S. have in recent years often devolved from honest disagreements and civil discourse into political sniping, "cancel culture," and efforts to silence opposing viewpoints. Many who claim the mantle of liberal education are in fact engaging in very illiberal practices.

  To be effective, advocates of a rigorous, fact-based curriculum must stand up to the venom, name-calling, and snubs, large and small, that characterize too many contemporary "debates" on education. In the field of civics and U.S. history, reformers must champion a curriculum that is grounded in original documents, demanding reading, open discussion, and assessments that are both rigorous and meaningful.

The stakes for the future of our children and our republic

Before we turn to a closer examination of what is meant by "the sacred fire of liberty," we summarize the key issues in civics education and the implications they hold for our children's future and the fate of our American republic.

Our nation is fighting a multifront war against an enemy that many of our citizens barely understand. Traditional and social media alike champion moral relativism, deny the existence of ultimate truths, and bombard us daily with messages proclaiming that what feels right and good is perfectly OK — despite mountains of evidence that the abandonment of academic standards has engendered societal decay. Americans must recognize that the education wars are in fact a conflict between very different views of American history, religion, and culture.

Today, weighty issues with profound implications for our republic are debated in a spirit akin to how we cheer on our favorite sports franchises. But while partisans cheer each perceived victory, the scoreboard shows that student performance on key measures of history and civics literacy are pointing to a loss for both sides. The basic sequence and trajectory of American history — and how effectively our institutions work for the good of all — are at risk.

Simply put, Americans cannot afford to let petty ideological differences distract us from the magnitude of the challenges we face and the solutions that are within our grasp today.

Drawing upon the wisdom of our first president

"The sacred fire of liberty" is a phrase from President George Washington's first inaugural address, a short speech he worked on assiduously and discussed with James Madison. In my days as an English teacher, I would have a heyday discussing this phrase with my students. I'd start off by asking about the way it connects American politics with the holy.

In pronouncing that phrase, George Washington began a tradition that was destined to go far beyond the customary invocation "God bless the United States of America." But he was not just asking for divine protection; he was claiming that our new political system actually carries out a divine purpose.

Some 50 years later, in 1838, a young but deep Abraham Lincoln, then in his 20s, said in his Lyceum speech: "Let reverence for the laws, be breathed by every American mother, to the lisping babe that prattles on her lap — let it be taught in schools, in seminaries, and in colleges; — let it be written in Primers, spelling books, and in Almanacs; — let it be preached from the pulpit, proclaimed in legislative halls, and enforced in courts of justice. And, in short, let it become the political religion of the nation; let the old and the young, the rich and the poor, the grave and the gay, of all sexes and tongues, and colors and conditions, sacrifice unceasingly upon its altars."

Lincoln makes Washington's religious metaphors even more explicit. We live, Lincoln said, under a "political religion," which was an odd pairing of words in a country that separates church and state. But both Lincoln and Washington exhibited a post-Enlightenment willingness to commit a daring heresy by combining the secular with the sacred. Deists both, their metaphors identified our secular political religion with the pre-Christian pagan rituals of ancient Greece.

The sacred fire that must never be allowed to go out was watched over by vestal virgins at the temple of Apollo at Delphi, upon whose altars animals were sacrificed. But on this new continent, instead of killing animals upon altars, our sacrifices will be to protect liberty with our own bodies and, more often, to subordinate our private interests to the public good — the chief sacrifice that good citizens are called upon to make in a republic.

Washington and the virtue of disinterestedness

Such disinterestedness was the chief theme of Washington's first inaugural address. He praised the members of Congress for their willingness to sacrifice local interest for the good of the whole — implicitly urging them to live up to this praise. He also took time to explain that he would accept no salary for serving as president. He wanted to be — and indeed he became — the very paragon of patriotic disinterestedness. He offered to members of Congress "the tribute that his due to the talents, the rectitude, and the patriotism which adorned their characters.

"In these honorable qualifications," he went on, "I behold the surest pledges … that no local prejudices or attachments, no separate views nor party animosities, will misdirect the comprehensive and equal eye which ought to watch over this great assemblage of communities and interests."

Note the phrase "local prejudices or attachments." It was a theme very much on Washington's mind throughout the rest of his life. It was to appear again in his last will and testament, where he bequeathed a portion of his estate "to spread systematic ideas through all parts of this rising Empire, thereby to do away with local attachments and state prejudices."

And where was Washington's bequest directed in order to achieve this patriotic goal? To education. The schools were to be the means of subordinating local interests to the common good of the federation. And the schools, under the watchful eye of textbook writers who copied one another, proceeded to carry out their appointed task.

By the 1830s, Alexis de Tocqueville wrote admiringly that: "In the United States the general thrust of education is directed toward political life. In Europe its main aim is to fit men for private life."

Building upon the legacy of the Founders

The community-oriented character of American schooling in the first century of the republic was the result of deliberate policy by political leaders in the aftermath of the Revolution. Benjamin Rush, a signer of the Declaration of Independence, thought American schools should offer a common curriculum designed to create "republican machines." His sentiments were similar to the educational views of Washington, Jefferson, Madison, and of the most important early schoolmaster of all, Noah Webster.

The schools were to be indoctrination factories for democracy, designed to develop critical thinkers and able citizens in a context of loyalty to the common good of the nation. Early schoolbook authors began a long tradition of texts that aimed, in the words of one successful early writer, "to exhibit in a strong light the principles of religious and political freedom which our forefathers professed … and to record the numerous examples of fortitude, courage, and patriotism which have rendered them illustrious."

The reasons for this communitarian emphasis were obvious to American leaders in the nineteenth century. Loyalty to the federation had to be developed in the citizens, as well as adherence to Enlightenment ideals of liberty and toleration. For without universal indoctrination by the schools in such civic virtues, they feared the United States might dissolve — as had all prior republics in history — through internal dissension.

Madison had stated the root problem in *Federalist 55:* "As there is a degree of depravity in mankind which requires a certain degree of circumspection and distrust, so there are other qualities in human nature, which justify a certain portion of esteem and confidence. Republican government presupposes the existence of these qualities and degree higher than any other form."

This was, therefore, to be a chief function of the schools. Madison's colleagues shared the view that because republican government is so precariously dependent on the loyal sentiments of its citizens, and because other, more selfish sentiments are always dangerously ready to assert themselves, the schools have a critical role to play, not just in affording equality of opportunity but also in inculcating the political religion of the nation.

Americanizing immigrants — and the Americans

The aim of schooling was not just to Americanize the immigrants but also to Americanize the Americans. This was the inspiring idea of the common school in the nineteenth century, built upon a combination of thrilling ideals and existential worry.

For all its shortcomings, the American common school of

the nineteenth century became a success, as did the nation itself. By the end of the century, we were educating, relative to other countries, a larger percentage of the population. That forward movement continued well into the twentieth century, such that in the immediate post-World War II period, the U.S. ranked first internationally on many educational measures.

But by 1980, a significant decline had taken place, both in the U.S.'s position internationally and by comparison with our own past achievements. Between 1978 and 1988, for example, the science knowledge of American students fell from seventh to fifteenth place internationally. And since World War II, the nation has declined internationally from the first quartile in reading to the third, dropping from third place overall to fifteenth.

The root cause of this decline, which began in the 1960s, was, by then, a decades-old complacency on the part of school leaders and the nation at large.

The roots of decline: European Romanticism and child-centered schooling

In the early twentieth century, existential worries about the stability of the nation had subsided. By the 1930s, under the enduring influence of European Romanticism, educational leaders had begun to convert the community-centered school of the nineteenth century into the child-centered school of the twentieth century. That process was complete by 1950.

The chief tenet of the child-centered school was that no bookish curriculum was to be set out in advance. Rather, learning was to arise naturally out of activities and projects. A 1939 critic of the new movement, Isaac Kandel, described it this way:

"Children should be allowed to grow in accordance with their needs and interests … Knowledge is valuable only as it is acquired in a real situation; the teacher must be present to provide the proper environment for experiencing but must not intervene except to guide and advise. There must, in fact, be 'nothing fixed in advance' and subjects must not be 'set-out-to-be-learned' … No reference was ever made to the curriculum or its content."

By 1950, with new, watered-down schoolbooks and a

completely new generation of teachers who had been trained in schools of education, the anti-bookish, child-centered viewpoint had taken over the nation's public schools.

By mid-century, thanks to an accident of history, the child-centered point of view had become an intellectual monopoly. Just when our schools were expanding to serve a rapidly growing population, the modest normal schools that had trained teachers were being absorbed as schools of education into colleges and universities.

The 1920s saw a huge expansion of education schools. Between 1910 and 1930, 88 normal schools in the U.S. were transformed into teachers' colleges to be staffed by graduates of the mother of all American teacher-training institutions — Teachers College, Columbia University.

The rise and 'triumph' of the Progressive educators

These hundreds of prospective teachers and professors of education had listened raptly to the lectures of the new theorists, including John Dewey and William Heard Kilpatrick. The latter was the author of the most influential pedagogical pamphlet in American educational history, "The Project Method" of 1918, which said that projects are better than books and lectures. By the 1940s, thousands of schools had already put the project method into place.

A video titled "Progressive Education in the 1940s" captures the spirit of the movement.

"For generations, public schooling in the United States followed a rigid, unchanging pattern," the narrator intones, after which viewers see children reciting Christian prayers, being drilled in their multiplication tables, and memorizing the dates of historic events.

The video then presents a supposedly more enlightened approach to education, one that depicts children engaged in projects including cooking, going to local stores, and visiting an airport to watch the silvery planes of the day take to the skies.

Kilpatrick, who spent most of his long career in education

at TCCU, is seen proclaiming: "We are trying to help the child learn to face actuality, and on this basis build his ideas, his character, his sense of self-reliance, of how to live and work with others. In a word, we are equipping the child to face his future by learning to face intelligently his immediate present."

However well-intentioned Dewey, Kilpatrick, and others may have been, the evidence suggests that the fears expressed by a man earlier in the film were justified: "It's all very well to teach my boy to paint pretty pictures and build a birdhouse, but he doesn't even know his multiplication table."

Good intentions gone awry: What the testing records show

What were the results? If a child began public school in 1950s, the effects of 12 years of schooling would show up in tests taken in grade 12, in 1962. The graphs that follow chart educational achievement from 1962 to 1980.

The first graph shows the results of the Iowa Test of Educational Development. It is not a selective test, but one given to every junior and senior in the state of Iowa. It thus stands as an important barometer of school and instructional history, and one whose results cannot be attributed to demographic change. Between 1962 and 1980, Iowa simply did not change demographically to any significant degree. The state, like the students attending its public schools, remained 98 percent white and middle class.

The next graph shows the trend of civics knowledge between 1970 and 1980 among high school seniors as measured by the National Assessment of Educational Progress (NAEP), known as the "nation's report card."

Unfortunately, NAEP has only assessed grade 12 civics knowledge three times since 1970, so researchers do not have a wealth of data to go on. The rarity of such assessments is itself a telling sign, for we can well imagine that ensuring young people understand civics and the history of these United States would have been the first thing that a latter-day Madison or Lincoln would have wanted to do.

Iowa Test of Educational Development Given to All Seniors in the State, 1962–1980

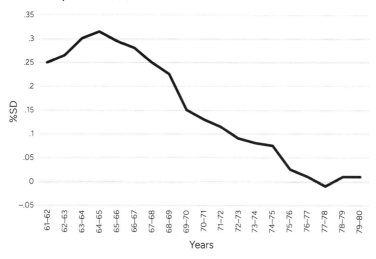

U.S. 12th Grade Civics Knowledge 1970–71 through 1979–80

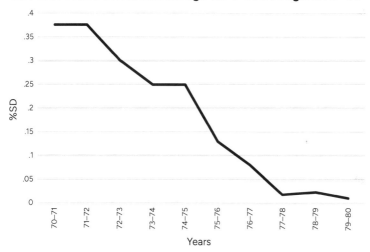

The downward trend in Graph 2 is clear. The significant decline in civics knowledge is important not just in itself but also as an indicator of the general change that was occurring in American schools. That so few American students know so little about civics reflects an irresponsible complacency about the proper role and functions of schools in democracy, as well as the more general anti-intellectual orientation of many public schools today toward what they consider "merely" academic subjects.

In the next graph we offer a story that many readers will be more familiar with, the decline of scores on the verbal portion of the Scholastic Aptitude Test (SAT), which was among the most important and ubiquitous measures of academic achievement throughout the latter decades of the twentieth century and into the early years of the twenty-first century.

The data show the steady decline in SAT verbal scores between 1962 and 1980. The data come from those students who attended elementary and secondary schools during the years in which Progressive educational theories came to dominant public education.

SAT Verbal Scores 1962–1980

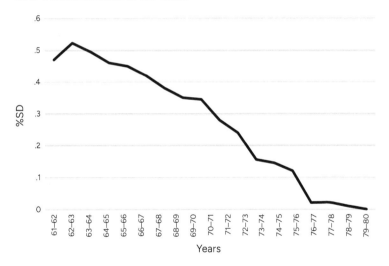

The sharp declines in the verbal SAT scores mirror the declines in the previous graphs. Together, they mark an overall retreat from the rigorous curriculum and rich content that once characterized American education.

Taken together, these offer a dismal picture of what happened to American schooling in the 30 years between 1950 and

1980. It is appropriately labeled the period of the great decline, and it is a decline from which America's public schools have not recovered.

U.S. 12th Grade Overall Achievement 1962–1980

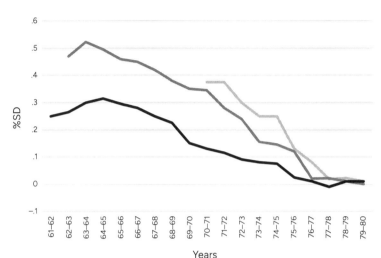

Forty-plus years of mediocrity in student achievement

But the news is actually worse than the foregoing data suggest, because the 40-plus years since 1980 — a time of remarkable advances in technology and cognitive science — have seen academic achievement remain essentially flat, showing some small gains now and again and declines at other times.

The decline in knowledge about "the sacred fire of liberty" was part and parcel of long-term decline in knowledge about all the other academic subjects learned in school, including science, art, literature, and history.

Our current education malaise is a national decline that originated in a national complacency that is foreign to our origins and best traditions. John Maynard Keynes said that ideas are more powerful than is commonly understood. "Indeed," he noted, "the world is ruled by little else."

American education started upon a downward path when the fuzzy ideas of Dewey replaced the hard-nosed ideas of Madison. To grasp that nettle we will need to show some intellectual daring. We will need to say that a definite, highly specific, and rigorous core curriculum — something only hinted at by the Common Core — is not after all an unthinkable idea.

It became unthinkable only when the complacent, anti-curricular movement began to dominate American schools more than seven decades ago. For the sake of their public schools — and the future of their republic — Americans had better be willing to think about it again.

■　■　■

This chapter is based on a talk sponsored by Pioneer Institute and given at Suffolk University Law School.

CHAPTER 6

No Longer a City on a Hill:

Massachusetts Degrades Its K–12 History Standards

By Jane Robbins, Will Fitzhugh, and Dr. David Randall

Thanks in large part to the Bay State's comprehensive school reform legislation enacted in 1993, history education in Massachusetts has fared better in recent decades than in the rest of the nation. Unfortunately, recent years have seen an erosion of the state's once enviable position as a leader in history and civics instruction.

The 1993 Massachusetts Education Reform Act (MERA) mandated core standards and assessments across all academic areas covered in the state's public high schools. The History and Social Science Curriculum Framework produced under this mandate and issued in 2003 contained strong, flexible, grade-by-grade standards for core knowledge, including the Greco-Roman and British roots of the American colonists' intellectual and religious heritage.

In February 2009, however, the state Department of Elementary and Secondary Education (DESE) suspended the 2003 history framework. And in 2018, DESE rewrote the standards to align Massachusetts' history education around service learning and civic engagement, a revision that seriously undermined the 2003 framework, which had been widely recognized as one of the strongest such documents in the nation.

This chapter offers an overview of how Massachusetts, which had long been a leader in history education, moved away from excellence to embrace trends that have weakened the study and understanding of U.S. history and civics across the nation. It outlines why state education authorities should return to the 2003 history framework, and institute a history MCAS test.

History Education in America's Public Schools

In 1991, Harvard University English professor Alan Heimert commented on the woeful gaps in his students' knowledge of history: "They are aware that someone oppressed someone else, but they aren't sure exactly what took place and they have no idea of the order in which it happened."[172]

Heimert attributed the decline in historical knowledge to widespread use of trendy social studies curricula that aim to introduce students to broad themes of human existence and behavior rather than factual knowledge about historical individuals and events.

The shift from history to social studies began in the early twentieth century with the rise of educational progressives in the mold of John Dewey. These believers in government by experts — rather than ordinary people — pushed an educational philosophy that shaped students for life in a collective society, rather than ingraining the knowledge necessary for full participation in citizen-directed government.[173]

This progressive, largely anti-academic philosophy came to dominate schools of education. Moreover, New Left historians offering revisionist accounts of U.S. history became a major influence in those schools — and academia in general — in the 1960s and 1970s. To paraphrase Ronald Reagan, those historians made sure that even much of the meager history that students learned wasn't so.[174]

For example, in *A People's History of the United States*, Howard Zinn offered a radically revisionist account of American history that focused on "class conflict, racial injustice, sexual inequality, and national arrogance."[175]

Early in the new century, federal policy changes further undermined history instruction. The 2001 No Child Left Behind legislation focused on reading and math, pushing history to the side.[176]

Another doleful influence on U.S. history instruction has been the Common Core national standards adopted by most states, including Massachusetts, in 2010.

Common Core literacy standards essentially require that English teachers teach history, and history teachers teach English — something that neither group has been educated or trained to do.[177]

Inappropriate demands on teachers are matched by inappropriate historical documents that Common Core recommends for teaching a "coherent, sequential and substantive" history curriculum.[178] Titles such as Julian Bell's *Mirror of the World: A New History of Art* and *Fedviews*, issued by the Federal Reserve Bank of San Francisco, are "out of place not just in a typical high school history class but in a typical high school curriculum."[179]

The impact of the Common Core literacy standards can be seen in the stagnation of National Assessment of Educational Progress (NAEP) reading scores from 2011 to the present.

Adding further to the confusion is the takeover of much of the high school curriculum by the College Board through its Advanced Placement (AP) courses.

The revised 2014 AP U.S. History (APUSH) framework, for example, is highly prescriptive, mandating that teachers work from a left-leaning, revisionist viewpoint that downplays America's strengths and achievements and highlights her failures.[180] A public outcry led to changes, but the overly politicized tilt remained.[181]

The situation nationally is dire, resulting in minimal, shallow, and slanted instruction that results in yawning gaps in historical knowledge. As the Pulitzer Prize-winning historian David McCullough once said: "I don't think there's any question whatsoever that the students in our institutions of higher education have less grasp, less understanding, less knowledge of American history than ever before. I think we are raising a generation of young Americans who are, to a very large degree, historically illiterate."[182]

History Education in Massachusetts: Horace Mann's Legacy

Massachusetts has a long and proud record of history education in the public schools. Reformer Horace Mann bequeathed to Massachusetts a public school system that was the envy of the nation. He also created a system of normal schools—named after the French *ecolé normale*—that offered professional training to men and women, broadened the curriculum, and discouraged corporal punishment. Massachusetts reaped the benefits of Mann's work for more than a century, with educational excellence helping underpin its economic achievements.

Nor did Mann's system neglect history education. Massachusetts followed the political insights of our Founders, who knew that citizens of a republic needed to know their history if they were to preserve their free form of government. Massachusetts required the teaching of American and general history in public schools from 1827 onward, and study of civil polity from 1857.[183]

Social Studies Replaces History Education

Unfortunately, the early twentieth-century Progressive educational movement subsumed the study of history within a social studies curriculum deemed to be more relevant to students who were presumed incapable of the serious study of history.[184] The serious study of history was given less and less time over the years, accompanied by less reading of original source materials and fewer demands on students to write lengthy essays.

Pushback came in 1993 with the landmark, bipartisan MERA, which required core standards and assessments in history and social science, including instruction "in at least the major principles of the Declaration of Independence, the United States Constitution, and *The Federalist Papers*."[185]

The 1997 history and social science standards based on

MERA focused on core knowledge, including the Greco-Roman and British roots of the American colonists' "intellectual and religious heritage."[186] In August 2003, the framework was revised to correct several flaws.

Grade-by-grade standards and additional content details were added, and more flexibility in sequencing was allowed for the high school curriculum.[187]

Anders Lewis and Sandra Stotsky, who were instrumental in drafting the revision, noted that the authors rebuffed criticisms that the framework should be less Eurocentric.[188] The Fordham Institute praised the 2003 Massachusetts framework for rejecting "the trendy cultural and historical relativism so often found in American education."

Warning Sign: The End of the MCAS History Test

But the first sign of trouble came just six years later. In February 2009, the state Board of Education "voted to suspend for two years all state history and social science tests, as well as the history and social science graduation requirement."[189]

State Commissioner of Education Mitchell Chester cited financial reasons, but a large majority of state legislators supported the tests and were willing to fund them. Although Chester and the board vowed to reinstate the history requirement "as expeditiously as possible,"[190] it remains in abeyance 14 years later.

Warning Sign: The Civic Engagement Initiative

Meanwhile, the Massachusetts Department of Elementary and Secondary Education (DESE) began to rework the K–12 history standards around "service learning" and "civic engagement."

While putatively nonpartisan, that revision was heavily influenced by progressive educational agendas and amounts to training students to be progressive activists—a misshaping of the purpose of education.[191]

Between 2012 and 2017, DESE commissioned a series of reports on civic engagement, learning, and college and career readiness. The goals outlined in these reports sounded innocuous — "civic intellectual skills," "civic participatory skills," and "plan strategically for civic change."[192]

But the content behind them was a different matter. At the University of Massachusetts Amherst, courses that contribute toward the Civic Engagement & Service Learning Certificate include *Grassroots Community Organizing*; *Marxian Economics*; *Embracing Diversity*; *Educating for Social Justice & Diversity through Peer Theater*; *Introduction to Multicultural Education*; *Organizing People, Power, and Change*; and *Race, Gender, Class, & Ethnicity.*[193]

Such overt political sloganeering, euphemized as "discussions of social change," informs much of the agenda of civic engagement as that term is used in educational jargon. This is what DESE was embracing in K–12 education, including in their revision of the history and social science standards.

New Standards on the Horizon

In July 2016, DESE began rewriting the 2003 framework. A review panel established two priorities: First, provide greater emphasis on civics; second, challenge students to "investigate, analyze, evaluate, and deepen their understanding of history, civics, geography, and economics."[194]

The document that emerged in 2018 repeated errors committed during the state's previous revisions to the science, English language arts, and mathematics standards, weakening their content and coherence.[195]

The 2018 history framework revision fails Massachusetts students and teachers in five critical ways:

- Where the 2003 framework organized its curriculum around coherent sequences of American and European history, the 2018 revision substitutes incoherent fragments that obstruct students from learning about historical progression.

- Instead of crisply written standards that were easy for teachers to understand and incorporate into their classrooms, the 2018 revision lengthens the standards by 50 percent and conveys them in unreadable education-school jargon.

- The 2003 framework provided a full account of our country's European past and its own exceptional history; the 2018 revision replaces much of that narrative with the history of politically correct protest movements.

- Previously, students were given sufficient time to learn European and American history; the 2018 revision abbreviates these curricular sequences, leaving students and their teachers with insufficient time, resulting in a deficient curriculum.

- Perhaps most importantly, the 2003 framework ensured that parents and the public could judge how well Massachusetts taught history by mandating a statewide MCAS history test. The 2018 revision eliminated that requirement and substituted meaningless expectations for each grade.

Authors of the 2018 revision justified their changes as enhancing civic knowledge, but the 2003 framework had already integrated instruction in governmental structure into the history curriculum, culminating with a U.S. Government elective in grade 12.

The real purpose of the 2018 revision is to promote DESE's civic engagement initiative, part of a national movement to replace classroom knowledge of civics with skills training for progressive community activism.[196]

While the 2018 revision still presumes that history and social studies instruction should consist of classroom study, it replaces the coherent, chronological study of history with a focus on civic engagement.

For example, study of the nation's founding period is subordinated to the civil rights movement. The revision bizarrely narrows the importance of the U.S. Constitution, stating that the civil rights movement "is the reason the foundational documents are relevant to all periods of United States history."[197]

Moreover, the 2018 revision dedicates an entire year to the ahistorical study of civics — which disorganizes the historical sequence of study and gravely restricts students' ability to historicize their civics knowledge.[198]

Why Massachusetts Should Return to the 2003 Framework

The 2003 framework organizes history standards in a coherent curricular sequence that covers geography, economics, and civics and gives students the historically framed knowledge they need to act as informed citizens.

- Elementary school introduces national symbols, state and U.S. geography, and proceeds to a historically integrated introduction to early American history and our mode of government.
- In middle school, students proceed from world geography to a study of the ancient and classical roots of our country.
- High school includes a coherent, chronological study of American and European history, integrated with economics and civics, and culminates with electives that highlight economic and political liberty.

The 2003 framework is characterized by sound pedagogical structure, abundant historical content, high expectations, and crisply written standards. In addition, the MCAS history test would have provided an incentive and assessment to ensure that students are actually taught this material — and to allow parents to judge the quality of instruction at their children's schools.[199]

Weaknesses of the 2018 Revision

The 2018 revision consistently uses politically correct vocabulary and the language of educational doublespeak. It is clear that contemporary progressive polemics animate the choice of words. The 2018 revision:

- Changes the 2003 framework's grade 1 curriculum, "True Stories and Folk Tales from America and Around the World," to "Leadership, Cooperation, Unity, and Diversity."
- Changes the grade 3 title "Massachusetts and Its Cities and Towns: Geography and History" to "Massachusetts, Home to Many Different People."[200]
- Eliminates the use of B.C. and A.D. in dates.[201]

- Refers to "native peoples," banishing the word "Indians" to a footnote,[202] even though many scholars use "Indians" and many Indians prefer that term or their tribal names, to "Native Americans" or "native peoples."
- The 2018 draft uses "enslaved individuals" in place of "slaves," despite the latter term being widely used for decades—by scholars and none other than Frederick Douglass.

The 2018 framework compresses so much important history that students cannot gain proper knowledge or perspective. For example, the history of early Christianity and the history of Byzantium are grouped in one unwieldy subsection.[203] Worse still, twentieth-century Chinese history eliminates the phrase "Communist Party attempts to eliminate internal opposition"; the Great Leap Forward and the Cultural Revolution remain, but with no mention of the attendant famine, Red Guard terror, and labor camps.[204]

The amount of work expected of students has also been reduced by the use of "one of" or "might." The 2018 revision requires that students learn about just one Progressive-era policy, where the 2003 document required study of eight such policies.[205]

The 2003 framework directed study of several post-World War I conflicts, including the Boston police strike, the Red Scare, Sacco and Vanzetti, racial and ethnic tensions, the Scopes Trial, and Prohibition.[206] The 2018 revision compresses these facts within a much longer list labeled "Trends and events students might research include."[207]

And while the revision drastically reduces the core historical curriculum, it devotes substantial time to material that suits progressive dogma but is of marginal historical importance, inserting mention of native peoples at every point, even where their impact on American history was trivial.[208]

For example, students studying the foundations of America's political system are now asked to analyze similarities between the "system of government in the United States and governing structures of Native Peoples (e.g., the Iroquois Confederacy)" — a largely irrelevant distraction from studying the American polity's

English, Enlightenment, and classical origins.[209]

Later American history requires students to spend substantial time on movements including those for disability rights and immigrants' rights,[210] but fails to question whether such concepts are more than current progressive polemics.

Distortions and omissions make clear the progressive slant of the 2018 revision. For example, a description of the social impact of the Industrial Revolution refers to "growing inequity in wealth distribution," which is questionable in light of a previous reference to "the emergence of a large middle class."[211]

At times, imprecision strays over the line to outright inaccuracy. The 2018 revision ascribes trial by jury to the extremely weak and distant influence of ancient Greece rather than to the direct and overwhelming tradition of England.[212]

The section on the conflict between tradition and modernity in modern America speaks of "major societal trends and events in [the] first two decades of the 20th century," but then cites numerous incidents from the 1920s, the century's third decade.[213] Independent of the question of interpretation, such errors of fact and wording weaken confidence in the 2018 revision.

Even on its own interdisciplinary terms, the 2018 revision is insufficient. For example, the discussion of archaeology as a way to understand prehistoric peoples fails to include the latest DNA research, which has revolutionized the study of early humanity.[214] If history should be taught in an interdisciplinary fashion, it should incorporate the hard sciences as well as the social sciences.

The grade 8 civics course contains basic errors:

- It identifies diversity—the current euphemism for racial quotas and their carapace of propaganda—as one of the "fundamental principles and values of American political and civic life."[215]
- It posits that the Necessary and Proper Clause "enables the Constitution to change over time through Acts of Congress" while omitting that the clause has been abused to allow

Congress to change laws that should only be changed by constitutional amendment.[216]

Curricular Organization

In addition to distorting the content of the 2003 framework, the 2018 revision distorts its structure.

- The grade 5 content states that the reason the foundational documents of early American history are relevant to all periods is rooted only in the modern civil rights movement and in the desire to extend "equality to all."[217] This reverses the relative importance of our founding documents and the civil rights movement and erases *expanding liberty* from the essential justification for our republic.

- The grade 6 and grade 7 standards replace a coherent history of the roots of Western Civilization with a hodge-podge of world geography and culture that teaches Sumer, Egypt, and Israel at the start of grade 6 and Greece and Rome at the end of grade 7; it asks that students explain why ancient and classical civilizations around the Mediterranean are described by some historians as the roots of Western Civilization.[218]

"Some historians" should read "every competent historian," since every competent historian recognizes the importance of these civilizations' confluence in the birth of the West.

The errors continue in the grade 8 civics course, which detaches study of the Constitution from a coherent sequence of U.S. and world history. Students should first learn about the constitutional Founding, followed by constitutional history. Specialized instruction in civics should come after that historical sequence, at the end of high school.

The insertion of the grade 8 civics course introduces inefficient repetition of material and, by compressing material, reduces by one year the time available for an in-depth study of U.S. and world history.[219]

The 2018 revision also inserts material on personal financial literacy — a worthy topic, but not one that should come at the expense of learning history, U.S. government, and economics.

Students taught by this incoherent curriculum will remain partially or totally ignorant of the chronological and conceptual links that unite Western Civilization. They will learn civics shorn of historical context and history shorn of civic import.

Pedagogical Structure

The pedagogical restructuring of the 2018 revision vitiates any remaining value. Where the 2003 framework emphasized mastery of content, the revision substitutes research, inquiry, and analysis, but free of any assessment to help lead to mastery of substantial content.[220]

Moreover, the 2018 revision expands the framework from 131 to 193 pages, so weighted with education jargon as to be practically unreadable. Neither teachers nor the public can be expected to understand the revision as well as they could the 2003 original. That loss of clarity itself degrades both democratic accountability and pedagogical utility.[221]

A history framework should also inspire teachers to go beyond their textbook and assigned primary sources to read specialized works of history on their own to deepen the history they convey to their students. The 2003 framework offered reading recommendations for teachers,[222] but the 2018 revision lists only websites and doesn't encourage teachers to read a single book.[223]

Most importantly, of course, the 2018 revision drops the 2003 alignment with the requirement of an MCAS history test, thus rendering its elaboration of expectations — carefully calibrated to each grade — pedagogically null.[224]

Each of the 2018 revision's failings is sufficient to disqualify it as an adequate standard for K–12 history instruction. Its many flaws — from overtly progressive distortions and omissions of content to incoherent curricular organization and a lax pedagogical framework — make clear that it cannot be salvaged, even in part. It should be rejected outright.

DESE should reconfirm the 2003 history framework and implement the 2009 history MCAS test throughout the state. Failing that, DESE should at least allow teachers and schools to voluntarily adopt the 2003 standards while a new committee drafts an entirely new framework and assessment.

What a New History Framework Should Look Like

Any new framework should model itself upon the virtues of the 2003 framework and embody the following principles:[225]

- Draft crisply written history standards
- Focus on content requirements rather than process concepts
- Preserve coherent chronological sequences for European and U.S. history with integrated non-ideological civics instruction
- Remove service-learning-driven civic engagement
- Align history standards with the 2003 framework rather than the inferior standards provided from the College Board or Common Core sequence[226]
- Integrate coverage of economic and political liberty
- Emphasize liberty, religious freedom, the republic, individual rights, and national unity
- Suggest primary sources that include balanced and opposing points of view
- Preserve civics instruction as a final-year elective
- Require mandatory assessments for both history and economics

Should DESE seek to add new topics to those provided by the 2003 framework, the following important content areas should receive priority:

- The role of DNA analysis in expanding our knowledge of human prehistory
- The historical development of Islamic belief before the emergence of the current version of the Koran *circa* 800 A.D.
- The development of bourgeois virtues in Europe and America as the cultural underpinnings of the free-market economic revolution

- The history of religious liberty in Europe and America
- The modern development in Europe and America of the architecture of knowledge, from art history to zoology
- America's shared twentieth-century culture
- The postwar rise of the American administrative state
- The rise of China as a peer competitor to the United States

To strengthen civics instruction, DESE should:

- Turn the 2003 framework's U.S. government elective into a required course
- Endorse the Civics Education Initiative, already enacted in 15 states, which requires high school students to pass the same test that immigrants applying for U.S. citizenship must pass
- Add a civics component to the MCAS history test, significantly more rigorous than the Civics Education Initiative's requirements

These recommendations apply narrowly to the expectations of a curriculum framework. More broadly, however, DESE should improve Massachusetts history instruction in several ways beyond a curriculum framework's remit.

Integrate Instructional Texts

DESE should provide suggestions for history and government teachers of specific instructional texts that could be assigned in grades 6–10 to prepare students to read a particular seminal text in grades 11 or 12.

For example, to prepare students to read *Federalist 10* in grade 11, students could be assigned Barbara Mitchell's *Father of the Constitution: A Story about James Madison* in grade 6 or 7; Catherine Drinker Bowen's *Miracle at Philadelphia* in grade 7, 8, or 9; and de Crèvecoeur's *Letters from an American Farmer* in grade 9 or 10.

Writing Expectations

Both the 2003 framework and the 2018 revision focus on the

subject matter to be taught. The 2018 revision greatly expands the learning expectations for each grade, but never concisely states writing expectations.

Any future framework should state briefly that history writing instruction should be integrated throughout the history curriculum to further the understanding of history, rather than merely as a component of language arts. Students should be writing nine-page history papers—research papers, secondary source analysis, book reviews—in grade 9, 10-page history papers in grade 10, 11-page history papers in grade 11, and 12-page history papers in grade 12.

These papers should demonstrate intellectual sophistication, knowledge of the formal apparatus of writing history, and knowledge of how to conduct historical research, and meet high academic standards of spelling, punctuation, and grammar.

Reading Lists

DESE should provide reading lists of exemplary works of historical scholarship for students as well as for teachers. Students should be introduced to history as a scholarly tradition and conversation and be aware that it is more than a textbook and a primary-source reader. Students should be assigned at least one complete history book each year in school — such as James McPherson's *Battle Cry of Freedom: The Civil War Era* (1988), David McCullough's *The Wright Brothers* (2015), and Taylor Branch's *The King Years: Historic Moments in the Civil Rights Movement* (2013).

History Teacher Licensure Requirements

Massachusetts history teachers should be required to possess a history major (eight courses), including a two-semester European history survey course, a two-semester American history survey course, an advanced European history course, and an advanced American history course.

History Teacher Professional Development

Massachusetts state government should fund professional

development programs for K–12 history teachers that center on teaching rigorous academic content. These programs should include readings and/or lesson plans from established, reputable scholars such as Gordon Wood, Joseph Ellis, James McPherson, and John Lewis Gaddis.

In an address to the National Association of Scholars in early 2018, Professor Wilfred McClay elucidated the purpose of a secondary school education in American history:

"It is a rite of civic membership, an act of inculcation and formation, a way in which the young are introduced to the fullness of their political and cultural inheritance as Americans, enabling them to become literate and conversant in its many features, and to appropriate fully all that it has to offer them, both its privileges and its burdens. It is to make its stories theirs, and thereby let them come into possession of the common treasure of its cultural life. In that sense, the study of history is different from any other academic subject. It is not merely a body of knowledge. It also ushers the individual person into membership in a common world and situates him in space and time. As in Plato's great allegory of the cave, it ushers him into the light of day, into a public world, into a fuller and more capacious identity."[227]

The Founding Fathers recognized that a democratic republic cannot survive unless young Americans receive this kind of history education. Disjointed and fractured stories, told from the perspective of identity politics and requiring little of students other than politicized dabbling in "civic engagement," will not bring any student "into possession of the common treasure" of American cultural life.

Failure to provide effective history education does an irreparable disservice to both students and the nation. The 2018 revised Massachusetts history framework fails to meet the standard for effective history education. It must be replaced with a framework that requires much of students but offers them, in return, a share of our common treasure.

CHAPTER 7

Advanced Civics for U.S. History Teachers
Focusing on the Founding Documents

By Dr. Anders Lewis and William Donovan

Introduction

The teaching of American history is becoming a thing of the past. Knowledge of our nation's foundational documents, seminal events, and pivotal leaders is in retreat. The problem, in a nation that has historically valued an informed and educated citizenry as the cornerstone of success, has reached — in the words of former U.S. Supreme Court Justice Sandra Day O'Connor — a state of crisis.

"We cannot," O'Connor once argued, "afford to continue to neglect the preparation of future generations for active and informed citizenship."

The crisis shows no signs of lessening. Year after year, fewer American students and adults can thoughtfully discuss the reasons for and the impact of the Declaration of Independence, the Constitution, and the Bill of Rights. A survey conducted by the Annenberg Public Policy Center found that more than one-third of respondents could not identify one branch of the federal government. Similarly, few students and adults can coherently discuss such seminal Supreme Court cases as *Marbury v. Madison*, *Dred Scott v. Sanford*, or *Brown v. Board of Education*.

The dearth of knowledge extends to American foreign policy. Most students and adults are not able to draw upon a wealth of knowledge to assist them in analyzing world politics and America's evolving role in the world. Few can offer an explanation for how America, a mostly isolationist nation through the nineteenth century, became a world power in the twentieth century, leading allied coalitions to victory in two world wars and playing the pivotal role in winning the Cold War.

When citizens do not possess strong knowledge of their nation's past, that history is prey for distortion and fabrication from both the left and the right. Conservatives mine our history to portray it as a unique tale of freedom-loving and God-fearing pioneers who spread prosperity and constitutional freedoms. Liberals often distort American history by portraying it as a tale of little else but brutal racism, unrivaled greed, and destructive imperialism.

What has brought about this state of affairs? There are many explanations, including the distractions of modern technology, a lack of state and federal support for history standards and assessments, and the dominance of amorphous social studies programs.

Equally to blame, however, are the ideas coming from the education establishment, including professors in schools of education, professional development organizations, and education writers and commentators.

Two of the trendiest are twenty-first century skills and "authentic learning." These concepts hold that learning takes place when students see how their life is connected to a subject. Otherwise, advocates contend, students become bored and disengaged, leading to the absence of critical thinking skills.

"By sparking students' interest in real issues that affect them and their peers around the world," writes education writer Suzie Boss, "you will give them cause to think more critically about what they are learning. Better yet, you may give them a head start on becoming tomorrow's problem-solvers."

The countervailing idea holds that the purpose of history education is to remove a student from the here and now and get them to understand ideas and worlds beyond their immediate interests. That view is anathema to those who back these trendy reforms.

That the stories of the past—the rise and fall of Napoleon, the career of Alexander the Great, the ideas of businessman John D. Rockefeller—might be intrinsically fascinating also appears to be beyond the realm of today's pedagogical standard setters. The notion that students want rich academic content—and do not wish to be treated as infantile adolescents—is scarcely to be found among most proponents of twenty-first century skills.

The near-universal acceptance of education trends can discourage young teachers who want to focus on substantive content. Several summers ago, one of the authors of this chapter attended a seminar on global learning and heard a workshop leader proudly declare she had reduced the time spent on the French Revolution.

"I used to spend three to four weeks on the French Revolution, but this year, I have it down to one day!" she said, adding that she focuses instead on contemporary French issues, including music, fashion, and cuisine. "My students," she declared, "just did not care about Napoleon, and I can't blame them!"

In 1996, E.D. Hirsch, Jr. wrote that "American educational theory has held that the child needs to be given the all-purpose tools that are needed for him or her to continue learning and adapting."

What is either deemphasized, glazed over, or absent, Hirsch argued, is content knowledge—the intellectual capital that students need in order to be successful citizens in our democratic nation.

More than 25 years later, Hirsch's words remain true. The terms and buzzwords change, but the underlying ideas of education theorists do not. But while self-appointed education experts persist with their theories, declining test scores prove that deep, substantive intellectual growth is not possible when schools avoid rigorous academic content.

Fortunately, many educators are eager for change. This chapter highlights four nationally known organizations offering teachers and students the opportunity to learn history in a rich, engaging, and rigorous manner — The Center for the Study of the Constitution, We the People, the Robert H. Smith Center for the Constitution, and the Ashbrook Center at Ashland University.

Center for the Study of the Constitution

Listen to any newscast, read a major newspaper, or visit a news website and you will likely soon encounter a controversy over the role of government. Can a federal health insurance program be imposed on the states? Are judges writing law and not interpreting it? Is the Fourteenth Amendment assisting illegal immigration?

The nonpartisan Center for the Study of the American Constitution (CSAC) at the University of Wisconsin Madison focuses on study of the 1780s, including the ratification of the U.S. Constitution and the Bill of Rights.

It was founded in 1981 as an outgrowth[228] of the Ratification Project, a federally funded program to determine "as completely as possible what the people ratifying the Constitution 'understood it to mean, why they ratified it, and what forces and issues were involved in the struggle over it.'"[229]

Since 2009, CSAC has offered a professional development program to help teachers better understand this critical period in American history.

"There's really only one issue in American history and that's federalism," said CSAC Deputy Director Timothy Moore. "Every one of the tremendous fights that we've had in our history has a federalism overlay to it."

The CSAC has typically offered three programs:

- A fellows program features scholarly presentations and discussions on the Constitutional Convention, with curriculum writing and lesson plans based on primary source materials.
- Thematic programs offered twice annually have dealt with topics such as the First Federal Congress and the urban judiciary.

- A weeklong summer institute welcomes 25 teachers who focus on the period 1763–1800, from the end of the French and Indian War until the First Federal Congress.

Topics for past conferences and seminars have included: "Political Humor and the Ratification Debates"; "The Challenges of Interpreting the Constitution"; "Limiting and Regulating the First Amendment"; and "Colonial Constitutionalism: A Study of Contested Sovereignty."

CSAC programs have a guest speaker in the morning who might discuss James Madison, the Bill of Rights, or ratification of the U.S. Constitution. There is time for questions and answers. Afternoons are set aside for group discussions. So, for example, a morning presentation on the debate between Federalists and Anti-Federalists over executive power might be followed later with discussion of essays supporting each view.

While the fellows program is limited to Wisconsin teachers, CSAC has welcomed teachers from across the nation to its other programs and seminars.

Moore said the professional development seminars for teachers at CSAC began for two reasons. The first was a response to the shift away from teaching government classes that emphasize the process of the legislature and how a bill becomes law. Rather, there has been greater interest in teaching government from a constitutional basis.

Moore said CSAC and others have also tried to fill the financing gap that occurred when the federal government backed out in 2011. CSAC did not want to lose its growing national network of educators teaching the Constitution.

Teachers who attend CSAC seminars tend to be older and more experienced, including many who teach AP U.S. History. But the organization also wants to attract younger teachers, many of whom have not adequately studied the founding period in U.S. history, which leaves them with a huge knowledge gap as they begin their careers.

"We're very committed to content and less so to pedagogy,"

he said. "We're heavily driven by primary sources and content. I think that makes us uniquely different from most professional development done in school districts and in the schools themselves."

Contact information:
The Center for the Study of the American Constitution,
UW-Madison, 432 East Campus Mall, Third Floor,
Madison, Wisconsin 53706.
jpkamins@wisc.edu, 608-824-0850.

"We the People": The Citizen and the Constitution

Like a well-prepared sports team, high school students who participate in the We the People curriculum program aspire to national competitions in which they debate the U.S. Constitution and the Bill of Rights. Their coaches are teachers whose professional development activities with We the People help them gain a deep understanding of American history and better prepare their students to participate in American self-governance.

We the People is administered by the Center for Civic Education (CCE), a California nonprofit, nonpartisan organization, in partnership with a network of 50 state civics, government, and law programs.[230] Funding is provided by state bar associations and foundations, universities and other organizations committed to promoting teaching and education about the Constitution and Bill of Rights.

Although some $10 million in annual federal funding for the Center for Civic Education ended in 2011, many state We the People programs have continued. We the People programs in Indiana, Wyoming, California, Oregon, and Virginia are particularly well regarded.

"I believe states ought to be doing this," said Robert Leming, the Indiana state coordinator and former national director of We the People. "Good teachers spend their entire career getting professional development just like any other profession. We require lawyers to do it and doctors to do it. You can't come out of undergraduate and think you know everything. You can't even get a master's degree and think you know everything in terms of the content. You have to continue that until you retire."[231]

The Indiana program offers several two-hour workshops each spring and fall, weekend seminars during the school year, and weeklong summer institute programs.

Leming said the model for a summer institute has three components:

- In-depth content concerning instruction in civics and government
- Master teachers instructing others in pedagogy so they can effectively teach upper elementary, middle, and high school students
- Performance-based assessments that require teachers to write, prepare for, and conduct hearings[232]

We the People summer institutes are week-long sessions held on university campuses. Content is taught by scholars of political science, law, and history, while the pedagogy is presented by master teachers who have considerable experience teaching the We the People program.

Unlike some programs, the topics selected for We the People workshops and seminars are frequently related to current events or perennially popular topics such as term limits or how to balance privacy interests with the necessary work of the National Security Agency.

"Jefferson said you shouldn't hold the new generation hostage with our ideas from the past," Leming said. "The Framers knew they were writing a constitution that could be amended for new generations to come. Obviously, they didn't know anything about drones and the NSA (National Security Agency), but we do."

The Competition

The simulated congressional hearing competition is unique to the We the People program.[233] Winners from state competitions go on to a national final. Roger Desrosiers, coordinator of the Massachusetts We the People program, said the competition is called a congressional hearing because in government Congress will typically call a hearing and people will testify on a bill, pro or con. Once they give their presentation the members of Congress will ask questions pertaining to the particular position.[234]

"I'm not a huge proponent of the competition for the sake of competition," Desrosiers said. "I am a huge proponent of the hearing process. The hearing process really distinguishes whether students have really grasped and understood what it is they've learned."[235]

Leming said the 2011 loss of federal funding had a huge impact on national professional development programs. Moreover, funding often goes first to programs in Science, Technology, Engineering, Math (STEM) subjects and not to teaching about the Constitution, a reflection of national priorities that have been in place for more than a generation.

"Sputnik did a number on the U.S.," said Leming, referring to the Soviet Union's launch of the world's first artificial satellite in 1957, during the Cold War. "When it went up, all of a sudden math and science became incredibly important and other subjects were put in a secondary position. Then you had the civil rights movement and the Vietnam War."[236]

Leming said that by the time he enrolled in college in 1972, teaching about the Constitution was not in vogue. Karl Marx was as likely to be the focus as James Madison. He thinks that changed somewhat in 1987 when the nation celebrated the bicentennial of the Constitution. From that increased interest in the Constitution, the We the People program was born.

Leming sees a renewal of interest in the Constitution in recent years because of perennial debates over immigration and immigration reform that often mark presidential campaigns.

Contact Information:
We the People,
5115 Douglas Fir Road, Suite J,
Calabasas, California, 91302.
https://www.civiced.org, 818-591-9321

Robert H. Smith Center for the Constitution

In the professional development program at the Robert H. Smith Center for the Constitution at James Madison's Montpelier, there is an emphasis on place. Located in the rolling hills of Orange, Virginia, about 25 minutes north of Charlottesville and two hours south of Washington, D.C., Montpelier is where James Madison drafted the Virginia Plan, the framework that led to the U.S. Constitution.

Madison's mansion, the furnishings, the grounds, the historic buildings, the views of the Blue Ridge Mountains, and the slave cemetery all contribute to a sense of an earlier time.

"Montpelier can be a pretty powerful place," said Jennifer Patja Howell, deputy director of the Center for the Constitution. "There's a lot you can say in a classroom, but when you are in the room where Madison crafted the Virginia Plan and looking at the view he had and surrounded by the books he would have been surrounded by, it becomes a very real and powerful moment."[237]

Founded in 2002, the Center for the Constitution seeks "to inspire participation in civic dialogue, improve the public's understanding of the founding principles of the United States, and enable citizens to deepen their understanding of and participation in our democracy."[238]

The professional development programs include annual seminars and online courses, as well as the We the People Summer Institute, in which teachers participate in a simulated congressional hearing.

The center covers topics such as the creation of the Constitution, evolution of American citizenship, and Madison's political thought, as well as programs on native peoples and the Constitution, and religious freedom.

Prior to arriving at Montpelier, participants receive primary documents to study ahead of discussions, such as writings by Madison, sections of *The Federalist Papers,* and selections from Anti-Federalist writers.

In additional to daily sessions, participants tour the Montpelier grounds. Teachers see the Old Library where Madison prepared for the Constitutional Convention. In the Drawing Room they find period art and conversation pieces. A discussion on slavery becomes more meaningful after they've viewed the slave quarters or slave cemetery.

"It gets their gears turning and they come back with more questions," said Emily Voss, former outreach and education manager at James Madison's Montpelier. "They come back with a lot of fabulous questions."[239]

"We use primary documents," Voss said. "The high school teachers find most direct use of that material in the classroom because we often will get AP-level teachers. The middle and elementary teachers are looking for big ideas. But it's largely on the teacher to figure out how they want to transfer those big ideas to their fourth or fifth graders."[240]

Just as Montpelier is used to stimulate deep thoughts and creativity about the creation of the Constitution and the Bill of Rights, so too is the work of James Madison. Teachers learn to appreciate the months of thought and writing that went into the Virginia Plan.

In addition, Madison's leadership in putting aside self-interest for the public good — a lesson often forgotten in today's highly partisan Congress — emphasizes that people can have a reasoned, informed conversation, speak their mind, and compromise.

"Madison didn't get everything he wanted in the Constitution," Howell said. "They deliberated and they had an intellectual conversation. The Framers decided to do what they could for the good of the country."[241]

Seminar leaders often address how teachers can raise controversial issues with students.

"The way we structure conversation around constitutional issues should be a model for how teachers can approach them in the classroom," Howell said. "But the additional discussion is that this is a topic that will ignite some passions. That's OK, but how do you as a teacher maintain the stance as moderator and not tell students how they should think about it?"

The Center for the Constitution's professional development program began in 2002 and attracts teachers from many states. There are scholarships available to teachers from donors and sponsors, including for teachers from Massachusetts, New York, New Jersey, Maryland, Virginia, North Carolina, South Carolina, Kentucky, Nevada, California, and the District of Columbia.

Since 2011, the Center for the Constitution has also offered online courses that include a forum for discussion. They are written by topic scholars, peer-reviewed by three other scholars, and range from eight to 15 hours in length. Teachers access the courses on their own time and can earn credits for continuing education upon completion.

Past courses have included:

- **Constitutional Amendment: The Bill of Rights.** This 15-hour course studied one of the most revered parts of the Constitution, one which, ironically, Madison initially opposed.
- **Constitutional Foundations.** This course examined the theoretical underpinnings of the Constitution, its creation at the Constitutional Convention in Philadelphia, and the three branches of government.
- **Creation of the Constitution.** This 15-hour course looked at how, after three months of debate, 55 delegates created a document that has lasted more than 235 years and yet has been amended only 27 times.

Another online tool created by the Center for the Constitution is ConText, a crowdsourcing project in which historians, political scientists, lawyers, educators, and others contribute thoughts and analysis on the Constitution, Bill of Rights, and other important documents related to their creation. Participants can browse the selected documents, read the annotations offered by scholars, and add their own observations or research.

Contact Information:
Robert H. Smith Center for the Constitution,
James Madison's Montpelier, Orange, Virginia
https://www.montpelier.org/center

Ashbrook Center at Ashland University

In the 1979 movie "Starting Over," Burt Reynolds, playing a college professor on his first day of school, works through all his prepared material, only to be horrified when he looks at the clock and sees that only five minutes have passed.

Officials at the Ashbrook Center believe that's a panic point that many high school history teachers reach. Understanding the arguments and principles that led to the U.S. Constitution and the Bill of Rights requires far more preparation than they receive in their undergraduate education.

"The education that our history, civics, government teachers get is almost always woefully inadequate," said Jason Ross, senior director of the Ashbrook Center. "What happens is they will get in front of a classroom and realize very quickly that they don't have the depth of content knowledge to make it through 180 days."[242]

The Ashbrook Center has been providing content and training for teachers of American history and government since 1989. Though the center was first opened in 1984 to host the Ashbrook Scholar Program, an academic program for undergraduate students majoring or minoring in political science or history at Ashland University, outreach to teachers began because of the perceived need for additional education in content.

Ashbrook provides professional development through a variety of resources and coursework.

- One-day seminars for social studies teachers explore themes in American history and self-government through the study of primary documents. Forums are half-day programs in which a scholar leads a group in an intense look at a single topic. The programs are open to K–12 teachers in public, independent, parochial, and charter schools.[243]

- Weekend colloquia are similar to one-day programs but offer greater depth and are held at historic sites such as Mount Vernon.

- Ashland University offers a Master of Arts in American History and Government, designed specifically for middle and high school teachers of history, civics, and government.

The program can be completed through weeklong summer seminars and live, interactive video conferences held during the academic year.[244]

- Ashbrook's website, TeachingAmericanHistory.org, offers an online document library with more than 2,200 primary sources from the roots of American government to the present.[245]
- Monthly Saturday webinars let teachers listen to panel discussions among experts and pose questions.

Ross said Ashbrook typically avoids lecture-style programs in favor of having teachers read and discuss primary documents, thus prompting them to think beyond a textbook.

"There are a lot of bad textbooks that teach a lot of mistaken things about America," Ross said. "We want teachers to have the knowledge and the confidence to be able to look at a textbook and say, 'This is what they concluded about this issue or this person, but based on my own readings, I don't agree with this conclusion.'"[246]

The goal, Ross said, is not to put teachers at odds with their school districts, but to gain a broader view of the nature of the American republic.

"We're very critical of ourselves today and we're trying to encourage teachers to look at the documents and use the documents as ways to engage their students rather than the textbooks which are typically going to a conclusion," he said.

Ross said that in education there has been a greater focus on doing assessments through "document-based" questions, rather than asking true-false or multiple-choice questions that "students of history and civics in particular find so mind-numbing."[247] He said there is an increasing emphasis on giving students passages to read, then asking them to pull out facts and draw inferences and conclusions.

"Increasingly teachers are being asked to focus on primary documents," Ross said. "They need to have more than the minimum foundation they get in their education. That's why organizations like Ashbrook exist."[248]

One of the goals of the center is to put an Ashbrook teacher — someone who has gone through its program — in "every one of the nation's 35,000 secondary schools."[249]

The school reports that during the past 16 years nearly 8,000 teachers from every state in the country have participated in Ashbrook's residential and online courses, webinars, professional development programs, and seminars at historic sites. Additionally, the school reports that during the past year 30,000 teachers per month have used educational material on the center's TeachingAmericanHistory.org website.[250]

"Our legislative branch has a less than 10 percent approval rating," Ross said. "That indicates something is wrong with our system of government. Most Americans see that people in Congress have a hard time talking to each other. We have a hard time getting past ideology and getting past disputes with one another. We have a hard time coming up with serious solutions to serious problems."

An Ashbrook teacher would be someone who has the depth of content knowledge they need and the confidence in their ability to read and interpret these documents so they can see themselves as scholar historians in their own classrooms, said Ross. By focusing on primary documents rather than lectures, Ashbrook-trained teachers can promote discussion and communication skills that are essential to self-governing in their students.

Contact Information:
Ashbrook Center at Ashland University,
Ashland, Ohio
http://ashbrook.org, 419-289-5411

Conclusion

Critical thinking is impossible without knowledge. And whatever the issue at hand — gun violence, immigration reform, climate change, or healthcare — true solutions require deep understanding of the law, human nature, and individual liberties.

Today, critical thinking about how we govern ourselves suffers because of a lack of knowledge about our nation's origins. Study after study shows shocking ignorance of the Constitution and Bill of Rights, yet without an understanding of those documents and the Founding Fathers' views, the principles at the foundation of our government are at risk of misinterpretation and distortion.

Politicians and business leaders often and rightly champion STEM disciplines, but our nation also needs a resurgence of interest in civic virtue and a new emphasis on teaching civics in our schools. There are two key challenges.

First, students graduating from college lack the deep knowledge of our government needed to teach it effectively. Second, there are too few opportunities for teachers to expand their knowledge once they are in the workplace.

The first problem exists almost by design. Liberal arts students may know key dates, figures, and documents from history, but few understand in depth the philosophical background and content of the arguments that took place at the Constitutional Convention. They need greater knowledge and appreciation of what Madison and others knew, such as the works of Locke and Montesquieu and their ideas on government and politics.

As to the second problem, seasoned history teachers acknowledge that most of their learning occurred well beyond college. Unfortunately, they may lack professional development opportunities or be required to take seminars that focus on iPads and smartboards rather than history content.

Fortunately, the programs discussed in this chapter continue to offer such opportunities, in spite of funding uncertainties, legislative inertia, and challenges such as the COVID-19 pandemic. Today, a variety of one-day, weeklong, and summer programs, supplemented by a wealth of online materials, are helping educators become more knowledgeable about our nation's founding years and provide an example of how to teach history to students.

The discussions central to every seminar encourage teachers to interpret the source material and share their views in an open and respectful way. At a time when gridlock is the norm in Congress, students can learn that in effective self-government communication is a requirement and not an elective.

Recommendations

In a 2012 interview with the *Washington Post*, former U.S. Supreme Court Justice Sandra Day O'Connor declared: "If we don't take every generation of young people and make sure they understand that they are an essential part of government, we won't survive."[251]

The crisis in the teaching and learning of history that O'Connor forcefully calls attention to can be solved but will require sustained intellectual argument and political engagement. Change will not be easy, nor will it come overnight. But with persistence and unity, history and civics advocates can restore the teaching and learning of history to its rightful place as a treasured academic discipline and fundamental educational priority.

Parents, students, government officials, and business leaders need to be made aware of the dire straits of history and the consequences of continuing along the path we now are on. Once people are made aware, pressure can then be applied at state and local levels to create and maintain the necessary academic goals and obtain the necessary resources to reverse course.

Pioneer Institute offers the following recommendations:

- **Require a statewide assessment in U.S. history** with a strong focus on the founding documents, given in grade 11 or 12 as a graduation requirement. As many of the educators in this chapter have noted, without meaningful statewide assessments, school system leaders in Massachusetts and other states will not make history or civics a priority.
- **Fund professional development programs** centered on the teaching of rigorous academic content. At the local level, administrators and teachers should ensure professional development programs include readings or lessons from established, reputable scholars such as Gordon Wood, Joseph Ellis, James McPherson, and John Lewis Gaddis.
- **Hire teachers who possess strong content knowledge.** School administrators often hire teachers versed in the latest pedagogical techniques but lacking in strong content

knowledge. In such cases, students might be entertained, but will not learn much of value.

- **Concerned parents and teachers should lobby school boards and legislatures** to bring attention to the crisis in history education. They should ask two key questions:

  - Is the local district's history curriculum academically rigorous and do school administrators provide enough class time for it?

  - Do local administrators provide adequate professional development time and funding for teachers to enable them to enhance their content knowledge?

Resource	Focus	Ranking
1619 Project Curriculum	K–12; limited higher education	F
1776 Curriculum (Hillsdale College)	K–12	A-
1776 Unites Curriculum	9–12; K–8 forthcoming	A
Bill of Rights Institute	K–12; esp. 9–12	B
Core Knowledge	K–8	B+
Educating for American Democracy	K–12 public policy	F+
FAIRstory Curriculum	K–12	B-
Florida K–12 Civics and Government Standards (Proposed)	K–12	A
Gilder Lehrman Institute of American History	all levels	B+
Generation Citizen	K–12	F
iCivics	K–12	D+
Jack Miller Center	teacher training	A-
Jonathan M. Tisch College of Civic Life	Higher education	F
Teaching American History (The Ashbrook Center)	teacher training	A
We the People: Citizen and Constitution	K–12 (9–12 reviewed)	B+

CHAPTER 8

Learning for Self-Government

A K–12 Civics Report Card

By Dr. David Randall

The ideological battle over school curricula began decades ago, and champions of a traditional understanding of our republic have been fighting back for a generation or more with textbooks, teacher training programs, and lesson plans.

In this chapter, intended for civics reformers seeking to defend and improve traditional American civics education, we review both traditional and progressive approaches to civics. We also assess the academic level of numerous K–12 resources. Many claiming to be for high schools are at best at a grade 9 or middle school level. The exception is Hillsdale College's *1776 Curriculum,* which is aimed at intelligent grade 12 students. None of the other curricula discussed here approach Hillsdale's level.

For quick reference, we offer summary grades for these resources, suggesting how helpful each might be in restoring a rigorous K–12 civics curriculum in American schools. Those offered by more ideological organizations receive Ds and Fs — not because they are incompetently written, but because they are all too likely to damage traditional civics instruction.

Introduction

In 2021, the American people awoke to a crisis in K–12 civics education. This crisis was not one of declining test scores and abysmal knowledge of our republic's structure and history, but the realization that partisans have imposed their political and social views. Critical race theory is one flashpoint, but subjects of dispute include action civics (training in community organizing) and other ideological distortions of the curriculum.

American schools traditionally have offered nonpartisan instruction to convey a broad account of American history and government. They sought to instill a love of country, build knowledge of government, promote understanding of each generation's contributions, and create self-reliant citizens.

The new progressive pedagogy instead advocates partisan education through revolutionary and illiberal departures from that tradition, including:

- Placing group identity ahead of individual membership in our republic
- Replacing the equality of individual opportunity with equity that aims for equal outcomes for every identity group
- Touting quasi-Marxist economics that discredit capitalism and free markets
- Advocating revolutionary liberation from an allegedly oppressive status quo
- Redefining intellectual inquiry from the collective pursuit of truth to the imposition of power

Ideological activists are committed to replacing traditional classroom instruction in American history and government with exercises in left-leaning political activism. The coalition Educating for American Democracy has catalogued many terms from these curricula, including *action civics, civic-focused schools, constructivist teaching, democratic competency-based, project-based learning, service learning,* and *social emotional learning.*[252]

The language may be impenetrable jargon, but the negative effects on traditional classroom instruction are clear.

Action civics, defined as "vocational training in community organizing," means students receive credit for work with non-governmental community organizations — reducing already precious classroom time. And action civics lets teachers impose personal views on students by influencing which community partners students choose to work with.

Generation Citizen, one of the more politicized organizations, states: "The road to a more equitable democracy begins with our schools… Through student-driven projects, youth learn how to effect policy change by engaging with local government and leaders to solve community problems."[253]

This progressive curriculum uses federal grants, national frameworks, state laws, school district policies, and classroom initiatives to prepare children for a more administrative regime that would divide them into identity groups rather than emphasize their common heritage as self-governing citizens in the American nation.[254]

The erosion of traditional civics began in universities and has migrated to schools of education, state bureaucracies, education trade groups, and foundations that govern American education.

The Jonathan M. Tisch College of Civic Life at Tufts University illustrates how this politicized approach is shaping civics education. Offerings include a civics studies major and minors titled "Entrepreneurship for Social Impact" and "Peace and Justice Studies." The Tufts Civic Semester is "a transformational first-semester program that combines academic and experiential learning with a focus on community engagement and social and environmental justice."[255]

Tisch Scholars for Civic Life helps students "… develop skills to take action for positive social change in community settings." Recent scholars' interests include "menstrual equity through service, education, and advocacy," "allyingship [sic] and participation in social movements such as Black Lives Matter, March For Our Lives, the Women's Movement, and recently, Stop Asian Hate," and "community organizing centered around gender equity, racial justice, gun control, and climate action."

For Tisch, training students for political activism comes before traditional civics study. But while would-be civics reformers must create rivals to such organizations, they should include studying the techniques Tisch uses to spread their ideologically driven agenda.

Educating for American Democracy

Educating for American Democracy (EAD) is the main force reshaping civics education toward action civics. Ostensibly for merely informing state and local standards, EAD's framework in practice seeks to force textbooks and lesson plans to conform to their vision of action civics.

A small amount of traditional civics content is included to satisfy more traditional members; the emphasis is on hollow educational skills, video games civics, and more progressive-leaning action civics.

EAD demonstrates the art of bureaucratic politics—the careful combination of putatively bipartisan compromise, impenetrable jargon, and euphemized but extensive radical commitments that will provide the framework to radicalize America's sprawling K–12 civics education. It further demonstrates that the radical activists' focus on political action does train them well in the arts of administration and obfuscation, if not to cherish and preserve a free republic. EAD encapsulates the America they would make—democracy and equity imposed and maintained by the Byzantine arts of career bureaucrats.

iCivics

Founded in 2009 by U.S. Supreme Court Justice Sandra Day O'Connor, iCivics began as an organization focused on providing actual civics resources for K–12 education. But in 2017, Executive Director Louise Dubé declared O'Connor's vision could not be realized "unless the country made a fundamental change in how civic education was viewed and made it a priority to educate students for American democracy."[256]

iCivics softly advances a progressive curriculum through

free educational video games that dovetail with the action civics pedagogy. These video games replace challenging academics, primary source texts, and expert instruction, with graphics, music, and student-led learning that contains soft biases.[257]

The game *Cast Your Vote*, for example, emphasizes civic engagement and green spaces. The game declares that equal access to public transportation is a priority, without focusing on maintenance, labor costs, taxes, municipal pension reform, or the burdens undocumented immigrants place on municipal services.

The other half consists of lesson plan modules geared to middle schools, with titles including *Limiting Government*; *Slavery: No Freedom, No Rights*; *Civic Action and Change*; and *Why Do We Have a House and Senate, Anyway?* [258]

While sufficient to constitute a comprehensive civics curriculum, iCivics offers no sequence by which these plans should be taught. The modular format encourages teachers to adopt individual modules into their curriculum plans rather than to adopt the iCivics curriculum wholesale.

iCivics also includes action civics lesson plans with primers on organizing protests and advocating for identity groups, including women, farm workers, people with disabilities, and American Indians. It never mentions right-leaning causes such as election integrity, the right to life, immigration control, or gun rights.[259]

Dubé helped craft the 2018 Massachusetts History and Social Science Framework, which replaced its excellent 2003 predecessor with a mixture of action civics and identity politics. iCivics and CivXNow work with Educating for American Democracy and assure readers that by 2026 all products will be "updated with an equity lens."

Analysis: The iCivics project disseminates a soft-progressive bias designed to force schools to abandon political neutrality and politicize instruction. Yet it is difficult to measure their impact. In 2021, iCivics claimed that "iCivics games and lesson plans are used annually by more than 140,000 teachers and more than 9 million students." [260]

Generation Citizen

Generation Citizen also funds and supports progressive action civics in selected states and school districts but spreads its influence by collaborations with larger organizations such as iCivics.[261] Generation Citizen embraces critical race theory, declaring that "systemic marginalization of communities of color and low-income communities has resulted in a lack of equitable representation and political power at all levels of government..."[262]

The organization would inculcate equity ideology and teach equity activism to "explicitly address the political and social marginalization from the formal democratic process that specific communities have faced." Generation Citizen holds up a catalogue of progressive activist groups as models, including Black Lives Matter and advocates of the DREAM Act.

Generation Citizen's curriculum framework asserts that BLM "elevates youth power and voice on issues that not only affect young lives but also our broader democracy, such as criminalization, racial equity, and mass incarceration."[263]

Bluntly stated, Generation Citizen aims to integrate progressive youth organizing into schools through teacher workshops, lesson plans, and curriculum.[264] The organization works to lower the voting age to 16 on the explicitly politicized grounds that younger voters are less white than older ones:

"By including 16- and 17-year-olds in the electorate, and experiencing the subsequent increase in turnout among voters in their 20s, the interests of diverse young people will be represented during a time of historic demographic change.[265]

Generation Citizen's list of action civics projects mirrors the progressive political agenda:

- Support for the Green New Deal
- Advocating school walkouts to protest gun violence
- Branding the Founding Fathers as merely wealthy white slave owners
- Pushing for school absences to let students participate in protests[266]

Analysis: Generation Citizen serves as a vanguard for action civics, showing how a broad coalition can offer templates for importing progressive youth organizing into schools.

The 1619 Project Curriculum

The 1619 Project Curriculum, produced by the Pulitzer Center, provides a distorted vision of American history based on the *1619 Project*.[267] Its biases include:

- Slavery was uniquely American
- Americans fought the Revolution to preserve slavery
- Lincoln was a racist intent on keeping blacks and whites apart
- Blacks fought back alone to secure their rights
- American capitalism was founded on plantation slavery
- American history is fundamentally characterized by black struggle against white supremacy[268]

The curriculum is narrowly focused like Generation Citizen but provides classroom lessons with a format that more closely follows iCivics. The curriculum provides relatively few individual and modular lesson plans, which are crowd sourced rather than provided by the Pulitzer Center. This approach relies on organic support — which appears to have been relatively weak — at the cost of coherence and comprehensive structure.[269]

The curriculum library includes *The 1857 Project*, focusing on the history of racial injustice in St. Louis, Missouri and Illinois, a unit on why migrants make various choices, and one titled *Buffalo Public Schools & 1619 Curriculum*.[270]

Though few in number, these lessons all claim extensive alignment with the Common Core standards, now adopted in many states.

The 1619 Curriculum's own lesson plans include a law school initiative, one on wealth, labor, and mobility, mass incarceration, and arts and culture. They are supported by the 1619 Project Education Network, which provides $5,000 grants to 40 education professionals to explore "key questions of racial justice and other pressing issues in a community that also includes award-winning journalists and the Pulitzer Center education team."[271]

Analysis: The 1619 Project Curriculum appears amateurish, the product of journalists, not academic professionals, and appears to do less damage because it is not crafted by experts. Its indirect effect is presumably more damaging, as education bureaucrats remodel standards to conform to its version of history.

Civics Education: Eleven Necessary Principles

A proper civics education should teach students about America's foundational ideals, from the foundation of the nation through the growth, expansion, and preservation of the Union. The following 11 principles are essential.

Ideals of Liberty

Schools must teach how liberty is embedded in the Judeo-Christian tradition, Greek philosophy, and Roman republicanism and continues with English ideals of self-government, common law, parliamentary sovereignty, and Enlightenment philosophy. They should study how liberty is secured in natural law and how America's forebears struggled to achieve ever greater liberty.

Constitutional Order

Our constitutional order was framed to secure Americans' liberties within an enduring republic built upon separation of powers, federalism, and the Bill of Rights. Subsequent constitutional amendments and judicial decisions are best studied as a history of how each generation has worked within an extraordinary constitutional inheritance to reaffirm natural liberty.

Expansion of Liberty

A knowledge of the Civil War and Abraham Lincoln helps students understand America's struggle for economic, social, and political liberties for all, and America's rededication to founding principles.

Preservation of the Republic

Understanding the survival of the Union as a moral imperative is essential to understanding what animated Daniel Webster, Andrew Jackson, Henry Clay, Stephen Douglas, the Compromises of 1820 and 1850, or why the Civil War was fought. Understanding how our republic works is useless without also teaching children to cherish its survival.

Expansion of the Republic

Our forefathers expanded the republic to make it more durable and better able to foster the well-being of citizens. Expansion to 50 states should be accorded fundamental importance in any course, as it provided Americans with the territorial resources for prosperity and greatness. Classes should teach students to be grateful to America's pioneers.

Commercial Expansion

Students should know that our nation fosters commerce and economic growth not as absolute goods in themselves, but only insofar as they serve the republic and its citizens' liberties. We support American businesses only insofar as they help sustain the republican order and do not decay into oligarchic malefactors of great wealth.

The National Interest

Territorial and commercial expansion are meant to serve our national interest, including the extension of diplomatic influence. Students should understand the threads that link the Monroe Doctrine, Roosevelt Corollary, our interventions in world wars, Cold War policies, and trade policies — and how they have served the liberty and prosperity of America's citizens.

National Unity

Students must understand the imperative of national unity and that the nation was founded by English settlers whose customs, religion, laws, attachment to liberty, and pride in the republic continue to shape us. Immigrants must understand that being American supersedes other creeds and ideologies and that Americans are members of a common nation, no matter their private beliefs.

Moral Crusade

Civics should teach students to cherish both America's predisposition to moral crusades as well as a republic designed to disperse and balance powers. Successful crusades such as the abolition of slavery and the difficulty of amending our Constitution both illustrate that Americans undertake fundamental change only when enthusiasms are general and enduring.

Populist Revolt

Civics classes also should teach students to cherish America's national characteristic of populist revolt, a necessary phenomenon given that our constitutional machinery cannot prevent the corruption of elites. A radical suspicion of government is itself an aspect of America's civic disposition. Our republic can grow brittle without regular populist rebellion.

Moderation

Moderation in the pursuit of justice and the defense of liberty is an eminently civic virtue. We should teach children that moderation helps preserve the republic, and that they must both tolerate and partially accommodate their fellow Americans when deep convictions differ.

Civics Education: Curriculum Sketch

The foregoing catalogue of civic principles requires a complex syllabus, with a varied cast of American heroes and sustained coverage of Colonial America. Students should learn about the birth of the nation, Puritan theology, English common law, and the Mayflower Compact. They must understand town meetings and colonial assemblies, farmers' conquest of the frontier, and merchants' search for profits on the seas. They should know about the self-made Ben Franklin, preacher Jonathan Edwards and the first Great Awakening, and pioneer Daniel Boone.

A civics curriculum should tell the stories of great figures — Paine, Washington, Jefferson, and Madison — as well as ordinary Americans who fought to achieve independence and adopt a Constitution.

By citing Abraham Lincoln, Martin Luther King, Jr., and Ronald Reagan, that curriculum should teach that crusades for liberty should be confident but never self-righteous. Students must learn the importance of national unity and cultural assimilation by studying figures such as Noah Webster, William McGuffey, Irving Berlin, and Jackie Robinson.

The virtues of populist revolt must be illustrated through the speeches of William Jennings Bryan and how Populists discomfited both Jim Crow Democrats and the Wall Street Republicans. The curriculum must also illustrate the limitations of populism through the careers of Huey Long, Ross Perot, and Donald Trump.

The power of moral crusade must find a place in this curriculum, drawing upon figures such as William Lloyd Garrison, John Brown, Carrie Nation, Woodrow Wilson, Alice Paul, and Jerry Falwell. Students must learn to be both inspired by and wary of crusaders.

A true civics curriculum should uphold the virtues of moderation in the exercise of national interest, perhaps best exemplified by Dwight Eisenhower, who practiced moderation both as Supreme Allied Commander during World War II and as president at home — the great compromiser who made his peace with the New Deal but prevented its further expansion while presiding over the apogee of American prosperity.

Finally, this unified, sustained civics curriculum should be taught across history, civics, and literature classes, helping students gain an integrated understanding of the civic virtues that have shaped American history, government, and culture.

Nonpartisan Approaches to History and Civics

Several groups articulate civics instruction that is nonpartisan and marks a compromise between advocates of traditional education and the radical establishment.

"We the People": Citizen and Constitution

We the People's textbook, also named *We the People*, provides comprehensive civics coverage, with a lucid analysis of the intellectual background, history, and structure of U.S. government. It is particularly strong on Greco-Roman history, Anglo-America law, natural rights philosophers, founding source documents, and key U.S. Supreme Court cases.

Analysis: The 2019 edition of *We the People* is well crafted and coherent, offering a framework for effective civics instruction. But while reformers can use it as a model, future editions should be made more academically challenging while retaining the focus on foundational principles and resisting partisan political pressures.

Bill of Rights Institute

With intellectual grounding in Enlightenment principles, the Bill of Rights Institute (BRI) "develops educational resources on American history and government, provides professional development opportunities to teachers, and runs student programs and scholarship contests." Dedication to the European intellectual tradition is evident in a lesson plan that compares Plato's *Republic* to Madison's writings in *The Federalist*. And BRI's materials evince a mild preference for free markets.[272]

This classic liberal focus, however, does not prevent them offering an engagement initiative that embraces the action civics movement. BRI's effort to embrace action civics for nonpolitical ends is laudable but unlikely to succeed. The civic engagement lesson, for example, cites the women's movement and the International March for Science but not Phyllis Schlafly or the March for Life.

BRI's *Yearlong Civics Course* provides seven study units, and the American history sequence — *Life, Liberty, and the Pursuit of Happiness*—has 16 structurally detailed chapters. BRI provides more curricular coherence than iCivics but less than *We the People*.[273]

Analysis: BRI has created a solidly crafted and moderately challenging curriculum, although marred by its inclusion of action civics. As with iCivics, its choice to focus on modular lesson plans allows for greater flexibility of adoption. Civics reformers should regard BRI as a good model, if not a stellar one.

Core Knowledge

Core Knowledge provides a range of curricular materials to support E. D. Hirsch's "knowledge-based schooling." Core Knowledge's offerings include *CKHG: A History of the United States*, whose materials are intended to support *The Pathway to Citizenship* and are crafted for a middle-school audience. While the material is solid, it could easily be used to settle for a "crib notes" approach that simply lists facts.[274]

While Core Knowledge's approach outshines the fact-free ignorance too common in American schools, civics reformers should ensure that civics education is always more than memorization of facts.

Core Knowledge's most interesting innovation is to tie its framework to the answers on the test developed by the U.S. Citizenship and Immigration Services (USCIS)."[275]

Analysis: Core Knowledge provides a solid middle-school curriculum in history and civics, which can serve as an effective tool for teachers, provided they use it with care. Another strength is its links to the U.S. Citizenship Test, since half of states have already passed laws linking their K–12 curriculum to the test.

Reformers

Hillsdale College: The 1776 Curriculum

Hillsdale's curriculum emphasizes natural law, the Founding, Abraham Lincoln, and the Progressive movement's deleterious effects on America. Building upon 2020's *The 1776 Report*, in 2021 Hillsdale published its *1776 Curriculum*, which immediately became the gold standard for high school civics.[276]

The *1776 Curriculum* eschews web-friendly devices of competing institutions, favoring comprehensive, lengthy text files that contain everything needed for in-depth lesson plans. This approach will attract teachers serious about teaching history and civics, although reissuing the *1776 Curriculum* in a more web-friendly format would be a service for other teachers and students as well.

The *1776 Curriculum* provides curricula for elementary, middle, and high school classes, repeating lessons for each level. While teachers and parents using it might do well to vary the lessons, the content itself is extraordinarily good and the only one among those we reviewed that will challenge intelligent grade 12 students.

Its selection of primary sources provides a thoughtful introduction to our civic past, including extracts from *The Federalist*, Lincoln's speeches, the Anti-Federalist "Brutus," and proponents of states' rights and popular sovereignty, including John Calhoun, Stephen Douglas, and Roger Taney.[277]

The curriculum's focus on the Founding Fathers and Lincoln—and abhorrence of the Progressives—leads to too little attention to other topics. Adding material on Andrew Jackson, William Jennings Bryan, and Dwight Eisenhower would provide a fuller canvas of American ideals and heroes.

Analysis: Hillsdale College's *1776 Curriculum* is by far the best K–12 civics curriculum reviewed, offering enormous amounts of essential material—the Founding, Lincoln, an assessment of some of the ill effects of the Progressive Era, and a fair assessment of Ronald Reagan. The high school sequence defies the almost universal degradation of academic standards in K–12 education.

Further improvements to the *1776 Curriculum* would be better adapting it for the web, making it more modular, and adding a textbook. Hillsdale can and should fix many of these flaws in time.

The Ashbrook Center: Teaching American History

The Ashbrook Center, an independent academic center at Ashland University, provides educational programs whose centerpiece is the *Teaching American History* graduate program, offering courses in person, hybrid, and online.[278]

The material includes *The American Revolution, The American Founding, Civil War and Reconstruction, The Progressive Era, Great American Texts—Heller & Vonnegut, Gender and Equality in America*, and *Indian Assimilation, Resistance, and Removal*.

Ashbrook provides its own edited selections of core documents covering the major periods of American history and debates pertaining to each. Historical and thematic collections include *The American Revolution, The Great Depression and the New Deal, Westward Expansion*, and *Religion in American History and Politics: 25 Core Docs.*

Ashbrook also offers toolkits that encourage teachers to peruse the collections for their own purposes. And while homeschooling is not the center's focus, Ashbrook provides a selection of lesson plans and resources that can be used by homeschooling families.

Analysis: Ashbrook's approach is a useful reminder that half the stakes in civics education pertain to educating teachers. *Teaching American History* makes the point explicit by focusing on graduate-level courses in a master's degree program.

Jack Miller Center

The Jack Miller Center has worked to strengthen higher education for a generation, particularly by sponsoring programs within universities that provide a traditional education in Western Civilization and American history. Its Founding Civics Initiative (FCI) now concentrates on broad-based support for teacher training.[279]

The Center has funded a virtual seminar series for Florida teachers, covering historical antecedents to the Bill of Rights, freedom of religion, and the Second Amendment, as well as funding for the Summer Civics Institute at the University of Virginia, Civic Spirit in New York City, and summer graduate courses at the University of Wisconsin Madison, Tufts University, and the National Constitution Center in Philadelphia.

JMC's support for the Civics Program for Teachers (CPT),

hosted by Lake Forest College, deserves particular mention because CPT "consists of a series of graduate courses designed to help teachers respond to the new State of Illinois civics requirement for high-school students."[280] Unfortunately recent changes have degraded the Illinois' civics standards.[281]

Analysis: Teacher training programs ought to be intelligently crafted to meet state standards, and the Jack Miller Center and its funding beneficiaries have taken a thoughtful and productive approach to meeting that challenge.

Other Programs

The following programs are representative of the many others available to schools today:

1776 Unites

1776 Unites was founded by Robert Woodson, Jr. as a patriotic and optimistic antidote to the 1619 Project.[282] Its *1776 Unites Curriculum* includes downloadable modular lesson plans that provide an uplifting version of black American history, featuring figures such as Crispus Attucks, Benjamin Banneker, Paul Cuffe, Biddy Mason, Elijah McCoy, Bessie Coleman, Booker T. Washington, and Alice Coachman. Other lessons include *Tulsa: Terror & Triumph*; *Jesse Owens & The Berlin Olympics*; *Resilience and Learned Optimism*; and *The Woodson Principles*.

The FAIRstory Curriculum

The Foundation Against Intolerance and Racism's (FAIR's) curriculum works within ethnic studies courses. While there is some question as to whether ethnic studies teachers will accept these materials, FAIR should be commended for making this effort.[283]

Gilder Lehrman Institute of American History

The Gilder Lehrman Institute of American History supports K–12 American history education with a cache of 70,000 primary source documents, along with curricula and lesson plans, although the materials are restricted to members rather than being open access. Its efforts parallel those of Ashbrook's *Teaching American History.*[284]

Florida K–12 Civics and Government Standards

The state of Florida has approved draft civics standards to restore more traditional civics. For example, they explicitly acknowledge the Hebraic and Christian roots of our civic culture and require the study of Colonial history. The standards provide a framework for each grade through grade 8, and then a detailed sequence for grades 9–12.[285]

Through consultation with school administrators and teachers, Florida's standards have been made more softly bipartisan. Reformers should note that no amount of civics materials in schools can do any good unless they align with state standards.

Elements of Comprehensive Civics Education Reform

Education Framework

Civics reformers should offer a roadmap, not impose a curriculum. Such a roadmap, with broad support from nonprofits dedicated to civics education, can provide a model for states and school districts.

Leveraging Higher Education

The Tisch College of Civic Life at Tufts University and similar institutions illustrate the influence that activists currently wield in higher education. Reformers should carefully plan long-term campaigns to reclaim traditional civics instruction.

State Standards

Florida's standards offer a template for reform efforts nationwide. Reformers in others state should seek laws empowering state legislatures to review standards and ensure districts can choose rigorous textbooks and curricula. Where districts already enjoy autonomy, reformers should defend that autonomy.

Assessments

In a perfect world, civics reformers could link reformed American history and civics curricula to rigorous statewide assessments, providing permanent incentives for proper civics and history instruction. The 2003 Massachusetts History and Social Science Curriculum Framework provided the best real-world example, yet bureaucratic resistance blocked implementation of a statewide assessment.

Many state standards are now hopelessly politicized. The College Board's AP exam in U.S. Government and Politics now includes an action civics requirement.

Civics reformers should seek assessments from competitors to the College Board, such as the Classic Learning Initiatives.[286] To succeed, such an alternative should link to AP instruction at a significant number of American colleges and universities and provide scholarship support for students who do well on these assessments.

Homeschools

Civics reformers familiar with homeschooling should lead the effort to offer resources to this market, bearing in mind:

- Homeschoolers already have many existing curricular resources, including self-generated ones.
- More explicitly religious civics instruction will usually be better received than in public schools.
- Modular lesson plans are favored by parents who often dislike standardized instruction.

Teacher Training

Civics reformers must first educate teachers and can turn to the Ashbrook Center and the Jack Miller Center for models. Reformers should also seek to transform teaching licensure requirements. Reformers should work within states' existing legal frameworks to provide proper teacher training — based on rigorous textbooks, curricula and lessons plans — that meet state licensure requirements.

Professional Development Support

Civics reformers should imitate the techniques of iCivics and the 1619 Project Curriculum that provide teachers with professional development grants. They should establish an effective eligibility screen since some teachers will accept money from reformers.[287]

Textbooks

Civics reformers need a coherent textbook to complement a resource such as Wilfred McClay's *Land of Hope: An Invitation to the Great American Story,* which provides a coherent U.S. history narrative. *We the People* and Core Knowledge provide useful models.

Curriculum

Hillsdale College, iCivics, the Bill of Rights Institute, and Core Knowledge all provide a unified civics curriculum, with Hillsdale's *1776 Curriculum* the most impressive for rigor and comprehensiveness. Reformers should develop a curriculum that emulates Hillsdale's in structure and is built around a textbook with a nuts-and-bolts explanation of how our Constitution works.

Thematic Curricular Units

Suites of thematic lesson plans are likely a more efficient use of resources than individual lesson plans. Philanthropists seeking to improve the effectiveness of reform materials should link support for teacher training courses to associated thematic curricular units. Commissioned textbooks should craft narratives that support natural jumping-off points contained within thematic curricular units.

Lesson Plans

iCivics, the Bill of Rights Institute, and the 1619 Project all provide individual, modular lesson plans; any civics reform campaign must do the same and can benefit by enlisting educators to provide crowdsourced materials. Yet it remains difficult to gauge the extent to which any existing resources are used.

In August 2021, iCivics claimed its plans are used by 140,000 teachers and nine million students annually but doesn't quantify how intensive or effective that use is. Civics reformers—and those financing their efforts—should create a textbook and lesson plans to support it, thus increasing the likelihood both will be used.

Primary Sources

The Ashbrook Center's Teaching American History and the Gilder Lehrman Institute of American History provide a wealth of American history primary source documents. The challenge for reformers is how to facilitate wide adoption of this material given low literacy expectations in K–12 education.

Far too few students and teachers can profitably read primary documents, and Common Core further inhibits genuine literacy in favor of remedial skills. Civics reformers must campaign for broader and deeper literacy and should demand that teachers take required classes in reading primary source materials, including training in how to get students to read such materials.

Professional Format

Civics resources should be designed with professional polish and crafted to be web friendly, varied, interesting, and age appropriate. Civics reformers should apply as high standards to the professional mechanics and marketing of their materials as they do to its textual content.

Common Core Requirements

The 1619 Project articulates how its lesson plans fulfill Common Core requirements. Reformers should not adjust their curricula and lesson plans to suit the academically mediocre Common Core but should create a template to easily demonstrate that their material meets Common Core requirements.

The Civics Test

Core Knowledge has tied its civics curriculum to questions on the U.S. Citizenship Test, which has been incorporated into public school civics curricula in half the states. Civics reformers should work to strengthen the USCIS test or at least defend it against being weakened or politicized. They may also usefully consider integrating the test's questions into their civics resources.

Multiple Strategies

Civics reformers will do well to align their efforts to make the most of scarce resources. But some independent reform efforts should remain so as to test new strategies per se. The civics reform impulse must not be allowed to stagnate through a process of seeking consensus and compromise.

CHAPTER 9

The Enduring Wisdom of the Founders

By Chris Sinacola and Jamie Gass

"Enlighten the people generally, and tyranny and oppressions of body and mind will vanish like evil spirits at the dawn of day," wrote Thomas Jefferson to the French economist and writer Pierre Samuel du Pont de Nemours in 1816.

Three years later, the 79-year-old Jefferson — author of the Declaration of Independence, and former governor of Virginia, minister to France, and two-term president — capped his illustrious career by founding the University of Virginia, which he considered among the most important achievements of his life.

Education was never far from the thoughts of Jefferson and his fellow Founders. The men and women who founded our nation understood that true liberty depends as much upon freedom of speech, thought, and religion as upon force of arms.

" *History by apprising [citizens] of the past will enable them to judge of the future; it will avail them of the experience of other times and other nations; it will qualify them as judges of the actions and designs of men; it will enable them to know ambition under every disguise it may assume; and knowing it, to defeat its views."*

–Thomas Jefferson, Notes on the State of Virginia, 1781

Indeed, Americans have long valued education — and Massachusetts has been on the leading edge of educational excellence since long before there was a United States.

Massachusetts' role in American education

Harvard, the first university in what would later become the United States, was founded in 1636, nearly a century before any of the Founders were born.

Massachusetts played a central role in the nation's birth through figures such as the rabble-rousing revolutionary Samuel Adams, lawyer and patriot Josiah Quincy II, and the printer and publisher Isaiah Thomas.

In 1828, lecturer Josiah Holbrook of Millbury launched the American Lyceum movement—forerunner of the Chautauqua meetings and countless adult and community education programs.

By the 1830s, Frenchman Alexis de Tocqueville captured the growing reputation of New England for educational excellence.

"In New England every citizen receives the elementary notions of human knowledge," he wrote in the first volume of *Democracy in America*. "He is taught, moreover, the doctrines and evidences of his religion, the history of his country, and the leading features of its Constitution. In the states of Connecticut and Massachusetts, it is extremely rare to find a man imperfectly acquainted with all these things, and a person wholly ignorant of them is a sort of phenomenon."

It was upon such fertile ground that Horace Mann introduced the nation's first public schools in the early nineteenth century, helping give public education — and education of the young in particular — a more central role in Americans' understanding of themselves and their country.

And it was in Massachusetts in 1993 that lawmakers on Beacon Hill, in the heart of the "Cradle of Liberty," added one more modest chapter to that illustrious history with passage of the 1993 Massachusetts Education Reform Act.

That landmark legislation that set the stage for 30 years of unprecedented educational achievement by infusing the existing system with new funding, standards and tests of academic quality, and the creation of public charter schools to provide greater educational choice and spur excellence.

Were he alive today, Jefferson could hardly find a more diverse and rigorous system of schools anywhere in America than exists in Massachusetts, even if it would not be quite what he had envisioned.

As historian Bernard Bailyn wrote in his 2003 study *To Begin the World Anew: The Genius and Ambiguities of the American Founders*: "Jefferson did not live long enough to see the dawn of a universal education for all Americans, nor could he conceive that a strange, unsystematic mélange of schools — public and private, parochial and secular — would one day create the universal education he so passionately desired."

A distinctively American education

But what would have surprised Jefferson and his fellow Founders of the eighteenth and early-nineteenth centuries seems to us today distinctively American.

After all, in the nearly two-and-a-half centuries since the Founding, Americans have sought to fulfill the words of the U.S. Constitution by creating a "more perfect union." Through a devastating civil war, decades of Reconstruction, waves of immigration, and the civil rights movement, our nation has drawn ever closer to realizing the vision that gave us birth.

Americans of the twenty-first century understand that the genius of the Founders lay not in perfection — they were far from perfect — but in devising a system of government with the strength and flexibility to welcome the unknown riches of the future while retaining the profound wisdom of the ages.

No guarantee of future success

But however natural such a system may seem, its past successes were never inevitable, and its future course cannot be guaranteed.

As the preface of this book notes, "without education as a unifying force, the Founders feared that the new nation itself might dissolve."

Few Americans in 2023 expect their nation to dissolve in any overtly political way. But internal dissension need not lead to a redrawing of political boundaries to undermine a nation. The path to national decline includes many other less obvious warning signs — the erosion of community, a coarsening of popular culture, the decline of patriotism, plummeting rates of voting and civic participation, and a loss of respect for religious institutions.

Each of the chapters in this book has touched upon one or more of the factors that have helped to forge educational excellence in Massachusetts and nationwide — as well as those that threaten to undermine the progress we have made.

But what are the implications of these trends? And what specific actions might communities, states, and the nation take to strengthen the quality of history and civics instruction and thus help ensure the long-term health of the American experiment in democracy?

Identifying the threat from within

In 1983, the landmark report *A Nation at Risk* memorably stated that "if an unfriendly foreign power had attempted to impose on America the mediocre educational performance that exists today, we might well have viewed it as an act of war."

It turns out that no foreign invasion was necessary. Forty years after *A Nation at Risk* sounded the alarms, the primary threat to American education — and American democracy — is not from without but from within.

While Americans endlessly debate ever-finer points of group and personal identity, stagnant test scores chronicle the slow decline of achievement. Instructional time is eroded by bureaucratic process, professional development activities of questionable academic value, and seemingly endless rounds of testing that subordinate assessments meant to guide and fine-tune learning to the goal of achieving a particular percentage.

Meanwhile, the culture wars rage on. In print, on radio and TV, and across the vast regions of cyberspace, educators, teachers, parents, and pundits alike endlessly debate the latest fads, score political points, and engage in public relations wars over the meaning and purpose of education.

None of that is any substitute for the rigorous instruction and meaningful discourse than once characterized American classrooms.

To be sure, most schools continue to teach something they label history, civics, or social studies. The content of those courses, however, is often only a faint echo of what students were once expected to know.

Reversing that decline will not be easy, but it can and must begin. And a better spot could hardly be found to do so than in Massachusetts, which offers a case study in how success can be achieved — and all too soon placed at risk.

Reclaiming the legacy of the Bay State

At many points in the preceding pages, we have spoken about the central role Massachusetts has played in building a strong educational legacy in the United States. The builders of the Bay State—figures that include John and Abigail Adams, Ralph Waldo Emerson, Horace Mann, and scores of inventors, entrepreneurs, and political leaders—shared a commitment to education.

Whatever their private beliefs and preferences, all were united in contributing to an enterprise greater than themselves, one that would endure for generations to come.

"Education, beyond all other devices of human origin, is a great equalizer of conditions of men," wrote Mann, whose pioneering work on behalf of public education in Massachusetts established a model for the nation.

In the more than 150 years since Mann served as the state's education commissioner, Massachusetts has built upon and expanded his legacy. But since the early years of the current century, warning signs have appeared suggesting that Mann's legacy is at risk. Educational performance has declined and that decline is accelerating.

Reclaiming a leadership role for Massachusetts will require new thinking among both voters and the politicians they choose to represent them. While a return to the spirit of the American Revolution would be ideal, Massachusetts can in the short term reaffirm its commitment to its own 1993 reform legacy in two ways:

- Follow the law and implement a U.S. history MCAS test as a requirement for high school graduation.
- Turn away from lackluster Common Core standards that have undermined the independence, rigor, and autonomy that states should exercise in education.

Rejecting the low expectations of Common Core

To quantify the deleterious impact of Common Core curriculum standards, one need only examine the ongoing decline in scores on the National Assessment of Educational Progress and other testing measures, as detailed at the end of chapter 5.

But to understand how far the quality of educational instruction has fallen over time, it is necessary to appreciate the extraordinary range of thought that shaped the Founders' generation. Adams, Jefferson, and others were immersed from an early age in the classics, from Herodotus, Thucydides, Plato, and Plutarch to Livy, Caesar, and Tacitus.

To the study of the classics, they added familiarity with Enlightenment thinkers, a knowledge of rhetoric, an appreciation for religious traditions, and training in writing clear and persuasive English. And the study and appreciation of history permeated their lives.

In contrast to the high expectations that prevailed even a generation or two ago in most American schools, today's Common Core is a lowest common denominator in education, an outline of the bare minimum students are expected to know. And as the dismal returns from standardized testing show, too many students are failing to meet even those minimums.

A better option — 50 laboratories of democracy

As important as it is to implement a history MCAS test and reject the low expectations of Common Core, more is needed. For civics to reclaim a central role in guiding the education of citizens — if it is to once more mold them into informed participants in a vigorous democracy — states must take seriously their role as laboratories for bold educational experimentation.

As detailed in chapter 4, many states have done so, achieving far stronger standards than anything contained in Common Core by exercising the autonomy granted to them by the U.S. Constitution and the federal structure of our republic.

Americans accustomed to the outsized role of the federal government in their lives may not realize that neither the Declaration of Independence nor the U.S. Constitution accords any role in education to the federal government.

Indeed, the words "education" or "school" appear nowhere in either document or in any of the 27 amendments to the Constitution. The Founders understood what too many Americans have forgotten: Some things are too important to be left to a centralized government.

Many in Washington, D.C. and elsewhere continue to believe that government is best which governs *most*. Driven by the vision of an all-powerful, centralized state run by technocrats and bureaucrats, they ceaselessly advocate for expanding Uncle Sam's presence in more and more areas of American life.

Education remains the province of the states

But education remains largely the responsibility of local and state governments, just as the Founders intended. And early twenty-first century America offers abundant evidence for the wisdom of the Founders' eighteenth-century vision.

Chapter 4 offers examples of curricular excellence that developed in very different regions of the nation, including Massachusetts, New York, California, Indiana, South Carolina, and Alabama.

While each of those states approached history and civics in different ways, they share key factors that informed a successful process, including:

- An inclusive and nonpartisan process for developing educational standards
- Attention to detail and clarity in sources and language
- A focus on academic content and accountability to measure progress
- Placing a high value on civics and the study of American history
- The encouragement of reading history, including original and primary sources
- An emphasis on having students write about history

These and other principles promote academic standards that have earned broad support and acceptance precisely because they take a bottom-up approach that involves parents, community leaders, and local organizations.

Simply put, the residents of a given community and state are in a better position to develop a rich and relevant curriculum — particularly for history and civics — than any national organization, never mind the largely political animals that inhabit the halls of Congress.

Consensus around the 'sacred fire of liberty'

In today's politicized and highly fractious America, even abundant evidence of success in one or more states may not be enough to persuade all of the enduring wisdom of the Founders. And even among those who are so persuaded, not all will endorse a decentralized approach that devolves power to the level of the state, the municipality, and the family.

Against that reality it is helpful to recall George Washington's first inaugural address, a speech that contains the famous words "the sacred fire of liberty."

In that address, Washington spoke of an "unparalleled

unanimity" that had helped create the nation. But unparalleled unanimity is not quite *complete* unanimity, something that our nation has never experienced.

In 1815, John Adams famously speculated that perhaps only a third of Americans had actively favored independence, while another third actively opposed it.

Historians have long debated the question of how many Americans favored independence. It is a point, like so many in our history, that can never be definitively settled. What we can say is that Americans of diverse backgrounds and opinions have always freely expressed their views, followed the dictates of their consciences, and founded schools in accordance with their beliefs — in the framework of a united and free nation.

Today, school choice and voucher programs continue to spread across the nation. Despite the heated rhetoric from the political fringes, true believers, and sensationalist media, most Americans simply want their children — and the children of their neighbors — to enjoy good schools that prepare them for productive careers and fulfilling lives.

That broad, sometimes quiet coalition of Americans transcends partisan delineations of left vs. right and Democrat vs. Republican. Its members understand that no one has a monopoly on educational excellence and that students can achieve great things in many kinds of schools.

They also understand, however, that too many publicly funded district schools — those that serve the majority of America's schoolchildren — are dramatically underserving those students. Particularly in urban areas, too many remain trapped in systems that fall short not only of the lofty ideals of Jefferson and Washington, but short of basic reading and math skills, and an understanding of the nation's history.

Reclaiming the American vision for all

Advocates for change must understand that excellence and rigor can never be achieved by rigid adherence to a single educational model. In a nation as diverse as ours, it can only be achieved by strengthening all educational models, be they public, charter public, private, religious, vocational-technical, or home-based schools.

In light of the growing understanding of what civics and U.S. history could be, it is disappointing to witness the actions detailed in chapters 6 and 7.

Despite being the direct heirs of more than 300 years of educational excellence, the Massachusetts Board of Elementary and Secondary Education has year after year weakened standards, including history frameworks, while ignoring the state law that requires creation of a U.S. History MCAS test.

Disappointments and signs of crisis can be found elsewhere, as well. As noted in chapter 7, a survey conducted by the Annenberg Public Policy Center found that more than one-third of respondents could not identify even *one branch* of the federal government. And few students or adults could engage in meaningful discussion of key U.S. Supreme Court decisions that have shaped our society.

Some blame too much testing, the media, or the distractions of the internet and popular culture for the decline of educational standards. Others appear to relish that decline, rejecting the received wisdom of the ages and following in the footsteps of a Howard Zinn as they catalogue the sins of the Founders, the legacy of slavery, and the alleged growth of inequality and injustice.

Today, many schools, from K–12 through college, pay more attention to alleged microaggressions in the classroom than to the obvious suppression of free thought and expression on their campuses. Books such as *The 1619 Project* purvey a history permeated by myth and resentment while the remarkable achievements of the likes of Booker T. Washington, W.E.B. Du Bois, and the Rev. Dr. Martin Luther King are relegated to footnotes or ignored altogether.

The hunt for implicit yet unconscious bias — concerning race, gender, sexual identity, cultural appropriation, or what have you — resembles nothing so much as the witch hunts that scarred seventeenth-century Salem and New England.

A coalition of, for, and by the people

Simply put, Americans cannot afford to continue along that path. And many are beginning to recognize that the disappointments, detours, and dead ends of the recent culture wars must not deter them from continuing to strengthen a coalition determined to reclaim our national greatness.

Members of that coalition can be found across the political spectrum and in every corner of the nation. Americans whose ancestors came over on the Mayflower stand side-by-side with new Americans from Africa, Asia, Europe, and Latin America.

They acknowledge America's imperfections without becoming paralyzed or jaded by a sense of historical guilt.

They recognize that filling school curricula with material that pays homage to every special interest and identity group may soothe feelings but cannot bring us any closer to understanding the causes of our national greatness.

They see that more than a million immigrants come to the U.S. each year — eagerly and legally — drawn here not by any light or transient cause, but by a deep yearning for the liberty they can find nowhere else.

They realize that the endless debates over education cannot obscure the fundamental truth that the American experiment in democracy continues to serve as a model to the world.

Above all, they understand that ensuring the future success of that experiment requires cherishing our past — and teaching our history to the rising generations.

It is only thus that we can realize the vision so eloquently expressed by Abraham Lincoln in the aftermath of the battle of Gettysburg, when he began to bind the wounds of a divided nation by declaring that "This nation, under God, shall have a new birth of freedom — and that government of the people, by the people, for the people, shall not perish from the earth."

.

Recommendations

For Any State Seeking Immediate Reforms to Its Existing History/Civics Curriculum

- **Adopt highly rated history standards** such as those previously used in Alabama, California, Indiana, Massachusetts, New York, South Carolina, and Washington, D.C.
- **Use the U.S. Citizenship Test as a requirement for graduation** from a public high school, admission to a public college, and eligibility for a Pell Grant or other public funds.
- **Administer the U.S. Citizenship Test to prospective teachers** so that teachers have — and students develop — the same history/civics knowledge demanded of new citizens.

For Any State Seeking to Develop Its Own History/ Civics Curriculum

- **Design an open, inclusive process** through surveys, regional meetings, and review panels, including outreach to parents and teachers so classroom realities are addressed.
- **Adopt a nonpartisan stance** that includes all viewpoints on contested historical topics and avoids giving excessive input and weight to special interest groups or activists.
- **Make standards and related testing materials detailed and specific** so that teachers know what they must teach, and students know what they should learn in K–12.

- **Focus strongly on academic content** and avoid education trends and fads, including so-called "21st-century thinking" skills.

- **Incorporate civics content that prioritizes primary source documents,** so students study the Declaration of Independence, U.S. Constitution, *Federalist Papers, et al.*

- **Require the reading of history in each grade,** from biographies to histories, so students develop background knowledge, acquire vocabulary, and understand historical context.

- **Promote historical writing** to help students develop clear, thesis-driven papers with strong analysis and use of evidence; increase the complexity and length of papers each year.

For Massachusetts

- **The state Department of Elementary and Secondary Education (DESE) should reinstate the high school U.S. history test** as a requirement for graduation.

- **The Legislature should require DESE to suggest specific reading texts** for grades 6–10 that prepare students for studying original sources as high school juniors and seniors.

- **To gain licensure, history teachers** should be required to major in history, with survey courses and advanced study in European and American history.

- **The state should fund professional development programs** centered on teaching rigorous academic content and grounded in the work of reputable scholars.

For Local School Boards and Parents

- **Establish remedial and enrichment reading classes,** taught by experienced teachers and volunteers, for secondary students who cannot yet handle high school-level texts.

- **Oppose the College Board's AP U.S. History curriculum** and push for U.S. history courses that unite students of all backgrounds, exemplified by Paul Gagnon's *Educating Democracy.*

- **Press local school administrators to explain history curricula** to ensure that they are academically rigorous and sufficient class time is dedicated to history and civics instruction.

ABOUT THE
Authors

BILL DONOVAN is a graduate of Boston College and American University, coauthor of *Investing Secrets of the Masters* (McGraw-Hill), and former Senior Business Writer at the *Providence Journal*. He has worked in media relations, written about socially responsible investing, and for the last 20 years has run Donovan Writing & Publishing. He has authored several white papers for Pioneer Institute.

WILL FITZHUGH is the founder of *The Concord Review*, the world's only journal for academic papers by secondary school students. Since 1987, he has published more than 1,000 history research papers by students from 46 states and 38 other countries. Fitzhugh writes and speaks about the importance of academic expository writing and the study of nonfiction books on history at the high school level. He holds a bachelor's degree and a master's degree in teacher education from Harvard University.

JAMIE GASS is Pioneer Institute's Director of the Center for School Reform. He has more than three decades of experience in public administration and education reform at the state, municipal, and school district levels. He appears regularly on local and national media and his op-eds have appeared in New England newspapers, *The Wall Street Journal*, *The Weekly Standard*, *The Hechinger Report*, *The Hill*, *The Daily Caller*, *The Federalist*, *Education Next,* and *City Journal*. Jamie speaks on education at events nationwide.

DR. E.D. HIRSCH, JR. is retired emeritus professor of education and humanities at the University of Virginia, and author of numerous books. His works include *Validity in Interpretation* (1967), a seminal work on hermeneutics. In education, he is best known for *Cultural Literacy* (1987), *What Your First Grader Needs to Know* (1991), and *The Knowledge Deficit: Closing the Shocking Education Gap for American Children* (2006). Hirsch is founder and chairman of the nonprofit Core Knowledge Foundation, and a member of the American Academy of Arts and Sciences and the International Academy of Education.

RALPH KETCHAM was Maxwell professor emeritus of citizenship and public affairs at Syracuse University, where he taught history and political science for nearly 60 years. Ketcham authored a dozen books, including *From Colony to Country: The Revolution in American Thought, 1750–1820, The Anti-Federalist Papers and the Constitutional Convention Debates, The Madisons at Montpelier: Reflections on the Founding Couple, The Idea of Democracy in the Modern Era,* and *James Madison: A Biography.* In 2003, Ketcham received the George Arents Medal for career achievement from Syracuse University.

DR. ANDERS LEWIS is a history teacher at the Advanced Math and Science Academy Charter School in Marlborough, Massachusetts. He previously worked at the Massachusetts Department of Education, where he helped write the Commonwealth's History and Social Science Curriculum Framework and create the History and Social Science MCAS test. He holds a master's degree and a PhD in American history from the University of Florida.

ROBERT PONDISCIO is a senior fellow at the American Enterprise Institute and previously worked at the Thomas B. Fordham Institute. He taught in a South Bronx public school and spent 20 years in journalism, including at *Time* and *BusinessWeek*. Mr. Pondiscio is the author of many books, including *How the Other Half Learns: Equality, Excellence, and the Battle over School Choice*. His work has been published in *The Atlantic, Education Next*, the *New York Daily News*, and *The Wall Street Journal*.

DR. DAVID RANDALL is director of research at the National Association of Scholars. He holds a bachelor's degree from Swarthmore College, an MFA in fiction writing from Columbia University, master's degrees in library science and history, and a PhD in history from Rutgers University. He has published young adult fiction as well as articles on rhetoric and the public sphere. His work has appeared in *Philosophy and Rhetoric, Political Studies, Telos, Modern Language Quarterly, Past and Present, Journal of British Studies*, and *The Sixteenth Century Journal*.

PAUL REID is a journalist and writer, coauthor with the late William Manchester of *The Last Lion: William Spencer Churchill: Defender of the Realm, 1940–1965*. Reid has appeared on C-SPAN's The Churchill Chat, was a Mason Distinguished Lecturer, and in 2013 was made a Churchill fellow at Westminster College. Reid earned a bachelor's degree from the Harvard University Extension School, was a regular op-ed writer for the *Boston Globe*, and was a feature writer for the *Palm Beach Post*.

JANE ROBBINS is an attorney and senior fellow at the American Principles Project in Washington, D.C., where she has worked to restore the constitutional autonomy of states and parents in education policy and to protect the rights of religious freedom and conscience. She coauthored the APP/Pioneer Institute report, *Controlling Education from the Top: Why Common Core Is Bad for America* and has written and testified extensively about the problems with Common Core. She is a graduate of Clemson University and earned a J.D. from Harvard Law School.

GILBERT T. SEWALL taught history at Phillips Academy, Andover, was on the adjunct faculties of New York University and Boston University and served as education editor at *Newsweek*. He has been a fellow of the National Humanities Center and director of the American Textbook Council. He is the author of *Necessary Lessons: Decline and Renewal in American Schools* and coauthor of *The U.S.A. Since 1945: After Hiroshima*. His articles have appeared in the *New York Times*, *The Wall Street Journal*, *Fortune*, *American Educator*, and other publications. His textbook studies include *History Textbooks: A Standard and Guide* and *Islam in the Classroom: What the Textbooks Tell Us*.

CHRIS SINACOLA is Pioneer's Director of Communications & Media Relations. Chris was a reporter, columnist, and editorial page editor at the *Telegram & Gazette* in Worcester and has worked as a freelance writer and senior marketing writer in healthcare IT. He is the author of photo histories of the towns of Sutton and Millbury, Massachusetts and has edited four Pioneer Institute education books. Chris holds a bachelor's degree in Italian studies from Wesleyan University.

DR. SANDRA STOTSKY is professor emerita of education reform at the University of Arkansas. She coauthored *The Rise and Fall of the Study of American History in Massachusetts,* Pioneer Institute, 2013. She is the author of *Losing Our Language: How Multicultural Classroom Instruction Is Undermining Our Children's Ability to Read, Write, and Reason, The Roots of Low Achievement: Where to Begin Altering Them,* and *The Death and Resurrection of a Coherent Literature Curriculum: What Secondary English Teachers Can Do.*

Endnotes

CHAPTER 1

1. *The Letters and Other Writings of James Madison*, 492, reprinting letter to George Thomson, June 30, 1825 (Lippincott, 1865).

2. Diane Ravitch and Chester E. Finn, Jr., *What Do Our 17-Year-Olds Know?* (Harper and Row, 1987), chapter 2.

3. National Assessment of Educational Progress results are reported by achievement levels: Basic, Proficient, and Advanced. For the most recent NAEP results (from the 2010 test) see "The Nation's Report Card: U.S. History 2010." Washington D.C.: National Center for Education Statistics. http://nces.ed.gov/nationsreportcard/pubs/main2010/2011468.asp.

4. "Most 12th Graders Know Little American History, Survey Says," *The New York Times*, November 2, 1995.

5. Sam Dillon, "U.S. Students Remain Poor at History, Tests Show," *The New York Times*, June 14, 2011.

6. NAEP. 2007. *The Nation's Report Card: Civics 2006*. Washington D.C.: National Center for Education Statistics. http://nces.ed.gov/nationsreportcard/pubs/main2006/2007476.asp.

7. NAEP. 2011. *The Nation's Report Card: Civics 2010*. Washington D.C.: National Center for Education Statistics. http://nces.ed.gov/pubsearch/pubsinfo.asp?pubid=2011466.

8. Intercollegiate Studies Institute. 2011. "How Civics Knowledge Trumps a College Degree in Promoting Active Civic Engagement." http://www.americancivicliteracy.org/.

9. Circle Staff. 2011. "The Youth Vote in 2010: Final Estimates Based on Census Data." *CIRCLE Fact Sheet*. Tufts University: Jonathan Tisch College for Citizenship and Public Service, 1.

10. *A Day in Third Grade: A Large-Scale Study of Classroom Quality and Teacher and Student Behavior*, National Institute of Child Health and Human Development Early Child Care Research Network.

11. Frances FitzGerald, *America Revised: History Schoolbooks in the Twentieth Century* (Little, Brown, 1979); C. Vann Woodward. "Fall of the American Adam," *Bulletin of the American Academy of Arts and Sciences*, November 1981, reprinted in *The Future of the Past* (Oxford, 1989).

12   Nathan Glazer, "In Defense of Multiculturalism," *The New Republic*. October 2, 1991; Arthur Schlesinger, Jr. *The Disuniting of America: Reflections on a Multicultural Society* (Whittle, 1991).

13   Howard Zinn, *A People's History of the United States*, 5th ed. (New York: HarperCollins, 2010); James W. Loewen, *Lies My Teacher Told Me: Everything Your American History Textbook Got Wrong* (New Press, 1995).

14   Gilbert T. Sewall, *Islam in the Classroom: What the Textbooks Tell Us* (American Textbook Council, 2008); https://historytextbooks.net/ED501724.pdf.

15   New York State Board of Regents, *A Curriculum of Inclusion*, 1989; New York State Education Department, *One Nation, Many Peoples: A Declaration of Cultural Independence*, 1991.

16   California Education Code sections 60040 through 60044, 60048, and 60200; the *Standards* add: "In addition to providing positive school experiences and encouraging students' aspirations, instructional materials should reflect a pluralistic, multicultural society composed of unique individuals."

17   For example, for U.S. history of the 1920s, "the student is expected to: (A) analyze causes and effects of events and social issues such as immigration, Social Darwinism, eugenics, race relations, nativism, the Red Scare, Prohibition, and the changing role of women; and (B) analyze the impact of significant individuals such as Clarence Darrow, William Jennings Bryan, Henry Ford, Glenn Curtiss, Marcus Garvey, and Charles A. Lindbergh. https://tea.texas.gov/about-tea/laws-and-rules/texas-adminwistrative-code/texas-administrative-code-title-19-part-2.

18   NCES. 2006. *Qualification of Public Secondary School History Teachers*, 1999–2000. http://nces.ed.gov/pubs2006/2006004.pdf.

19   Diane Ravitch. (1998). "Who Prepares our History Teachers? Who Should Prepare our History Teachers?" *The History Teacher*, 31.

20   In a comprehensive review of research on project-based learning (PBL), Thomas found that "most teachers will find aspects of PBL planning, management, or assessment fairly challenging" and "that students have difficulties benefiting from self-directed situations, especially in complex projects" (p. 36). John Thomas, A review of research on project-based learning, Autodesk Foundation, March 2000. http://www.bie.org/research/study/review_of_project_based_learning_2000.

21 Willingham, Daniel T., *Why Students Don't Like School: A Cognitive Scientist Answers Questions About How the Mind Works and What it Means for the Classroom* (Jossey-Bass, 2009).

22 Jerry L. Martin, "The University as Agent of Social Transformation: The Postmodern Argument Considered," in Howard Dickman, ed., *The Imperiled Academy* (Transaction, 1993), 203–209.

23 Mark Bauerlein, "Online Literacy Is a Lesser Kind," *The Chronicle Review*, September 19, 2008; Susan Greenfield, http://www.newscientist.com/article/mg21128236.400-susan-greenfield-living- online-is-changing-our-brains.html.

24 http://edsitement.neh.gov/.

25 http://www.discoveryeducation.com/.

26 The Federal Register asked for "…projects that address traditional American history, meaning for example, projects that teach the significant issues, episodes, and turning points in the history of the United States, and how the words and deeds of individual Americans have determined the course of our Nation."

27 http://www2.ed.gov/rschstat/eval/teaching/us-history/teaching.pdf.

28 *National Standards for Civics and Government*, Center for Civic Education, 1994.

29 Both the program (offered in many states) and the competition have been funded by Congressional appropriations and have drawn on an advisory board of prominent citizens and members of the legislative and judicial branches of the federal and state government.

30 Paul Gagnon, ed. *Historical Literacy: The Case for History in American Education* (Macmillan, 1989).

31 Paul Gagnon, *Democracy's Untold Story* (American Federation of Teachers, 1987); Gilbert T. Sewall, *American History Textbooks: An Assessment of Quality* (Educational Excellence Network, 1987).

32 Chester E. Finn, Jr. Foreword to *The State of State English Standards* by Sandra Stotsky (Thomas B. Fordham Institute, 2005), 5.

33 Gary B. Nash, University of Maryland Bradley Symposium on Multiculturalism, 1992.

34 http://www.aft.org/newspubs/periodicals/ae/fall2003/gagnon.cfm.

35 http://www.edexcellence.net/publications/the-state-of-state-us. html.

CHAPTER 2

36 We do not have data on the performance of Massachusetts students on U.S. history tests, in contrast to many years of state assessment data in English and mathematics. However, based on NAEP data and the neglect of history education by the state, we have no empirical basis for assuming that Massachusetts students are performing in history at significantly higher levels than their peers in other states.

37 Quoted in Paul Gagnon, ed. *Historical Literacy: The Case for History in American Education* (Boston: Houghton Mifflin, 1989), 112.

38 Richard Beeman, *Plain, Honest Men: The Making of the Constitution* (New York: Random House, 2010), 412.

39 Horace Mann, 12th Annual Report to the Massachusetts State Board of Education (1848); published in Life and Works of Horace Mann Vol. III, (1868) edited by Mary Mann, 669.

40 Gagnon, *Historical Literacy*, 112.

41 Diane Ravitch and Chester Finn, *What Do Our 17-Year-Olds Know?* (New York: Harper and Row, 1987), chapter 2.

42 NAEP results are reported by achievement levels: Basic, Proficient, and Advanced. See "The Nation's Report Card: U.S. History 2010." National Center for Education Statistics. http://nces.ed.gov/nationsreportcard/pubs/main2010/2011468.asp.

43 "Most 12th Graders Know Little American History, Survey Says," *The New York Times*, November 2, 1995.

44 See the NAEP report mentioned in endnote 2. Also see Sam Dillon, "U.S. Students Remain Poor at History, Tests Show," *The New York Times*, June 14, 2011.

45 Some scholars have turned Americans' lack of historical knowledge into a virtual industry by selling books to adults who realize that they have a limited understanding of their own nation. Kenneth Davis, for example, has authored *Don't Know Much About History: Everything You Need to Know About American History and Never Asked* (New York: Harper Collins, 2003) and *Don't Know Much About the Presidents* (New York: Harper Collins, 2012).

46 Mark Bauerlein, *The Dumbest Generation: How the Digital Age Stupefies Young Americans and Jeopardizes Our Future (Or, Don 't Trust Anyone Under 30)* (New York: Tarcher Perigee, 2009), 10.

47 http://www.kff.org/entmedia/mh012010pkg.cfm.

48 J. Martin Rochester, "The Training of Idiots: Civics Education in America's Schools," in *Where did Social Studies Go Wrong?*, ed. James Leming, Lucien Ellington, and Kathleen Porter (Maryland: Fordham Foundation, 2003), 28.

49 Sandra Stotsky, *The Stealth Curriculum: Manipulating America's History Teachers.* (Washington, D.C.: Thomas B. Fordham Institute, 2004). http://www.edexcellence.net/publications/stealth.html.

50 Paul Hollander, ed., *Understanding Anti-Americanism: Its Origins and Impact at Home and Abroad* (Chicago: Ivan Dee, 2004), 23–28.

51 Stanley Fish, *Save the World on Your Own Time* (New York: Oxford University Press, 2008), 12–13.

52 *A Nation at Risk* may be found at https://edreform.com/wp-content/uploads/2013/02/A_Nation_At_Risk_1983.pdf.

53 Gagnon, *Historical Literacy*, 10.

54 Bush's education objective is quoted in Gary Nash, Charlotte Crabtree, and Ross Dunn, *History on Trial: Culture Wars and the Teaching of the Past* (New York: Alfred Knopf, 1997), 150.

55 Ibid, 152.

56 Lynne Cheney, "The End of History," *The Wall Street Journal*, October 20, 1994. Also see Lynne Cheney, *Telling the Truth: Why Our Culture and Our Country Have Stopped Making Sense — and What We Can Do about It* (New York: Touchstone, 1996).

57 See https://malegislature.gov/Laws/GeneralLaws/PartI/TitleXII/Chapter69.

58 See https://malegislature.gov/Laws/GeneralLaws/PartI/TitleXII/Chapter69/Section1D. https://malegislature.gov/Laws/GeneralLaws/PartI/TitleXII/Chapter71/Section2.

59 For background, see Cara Stillings Candal and Ken Ardon, *A Changing Bureaucracy: The History of the Massachusetts Department of Elementary and Secondary Education.* https://pioneerinstitute.org/pioneer-research/academic-standards-pioneer-research/a-changing-bureaucracy-the-history-of-the-

massachusetts-department-of-elementary-and-secondary-education/.

60 See https://www.doe.mass.edu/frameworks/hss/1997/full.pdf.

61 From "How Should American Students Understand their Civic Culture? The Continuing Battle over the 2002 Massachusetts History and Social Science Curriculum Framework," in *Estudios sobre Educacion*, 2003 (5).

62 The 2002 framework can be found at https://www.doe.mass.edu/search.html#q=2002%20History%20framework&sort=relevancy.

63 Sheldon Stern, *Effective State Standards for U.S. History: A 2003 Report Card*. Fordham Institute. See https://fordhaminstitute.org/national/research/effective-state-standards-us-history-2003-report-card.

64 Diane Ravitch, *The Language Police: How Pressure Groups Restrict What Students Learn* (New York: Vintage Books, 2003), 138.

65 October 2006 meeting minutes at https://www.doe.mass.edu/bese/docs/?section=archive.

66 Kevin Dwyer email to Anders Lewis, October 2, 2012.

67 February 2009 minutes at https://archives.lib.state.ma.us/handle/2452/39094. Chester's letter is available at http://www.doe.mass.edu/news/news.aspx?id=4597.

68 May 2011 Massachusetts Board of Education minutes at https://www.doe.mass.edu/bese/docs/?section=archive.

69 Kevin Dwyer email to Anders Lewis, October 2, 2012.

70 See *Massachusetts Council for the Social Studies Newsletter* (Winter 2012) at https://www.masscouncil.org/?page_id=808.

71 Ibid.

72 Ibid.

73 See http://www.masscouncil.org/?p=2214.

74 See http://pioneerinstitute.org/download/pioneer-institute-report-on-history-in-schools/.

75 Pioneer Institute Report on History in Schools, May 10, 2012.

76 See Sandra Stotsky, *The Death and Resurrection of a Coherent Literature Curriculum* (Rowman & Littlefield, 2012) for an example of a coherent sequence of well-written informational texts from grades 6–10, 132–136.

CHAPTER 3

77 Madison to William T. Barry, Aug. 4, 1822; in R. Ketcham, ed., *Selected Writings of James Madison* (Indianapolis, 2009), 310.

78 All Together Now: Collaboration and Innovation for Youth Engagement: The Report of the Commission on Youth Voting and Civic Knowledge: https://circle.tufts.edu/sites/default/files/2020-01/all_together_now_commission_report_2013.pdf.

79 Surbhi Godsay, Whitney Henderson, Peter Levine, and Josh Littenberg Tobias, "State Civic Education Requirements," 1–2. http://files.eric.ed.gov/fulltext/ED536256.pdf.

80 *Christian Science Monitor*, September 17, 2008.

81 *The Daily Beast*, July 1, 2011.

82 The Nation's Report Card: U.S. History 2010: National Assessment of Education Progress at Grades 4, 8, 12. http://nces.ed.gov/pubsearch/pubsinfo.asp?pubid=2011468.

83 Stotsky and Lewis, *The Rise and Fall of the Study of American History in Massachusetts*.

84 Sarah Mondale, ed., 2001, *School: The Story of American Public Education* (Boston: Beacon Press), 22–25.

85 Diane Ravitch, "The Plight of History in Schools" in Paul Gagnon, ed., *Historical Literacy: The Case for History in American Education* (Boston: Houghton Mifflin, 1989), 61.

86 Diane Ravitch, "A Brief History of Social Studies," in James Leming, Lucien Ellington, and Kathleen Porter, ed., Where Did Social Studies Go Wrong? (Marlboro: Thomas Fordham Foundation, 2003), 2–3.

87 Diane Ravitch, *Left Back: A Century of Failed School Reforms* (New York: Simon and Schuster), 123–127. Gagnon, *Historical Literacy*, 4. Also see E.D. Hirsch, *The Making of Americans*.

88 Mondale, *School*, 98.

89 Mondale, *School*, 63–64. See also Patricia Albjerg Graham, "Assimilation, Adjustment, and Access: An Antiquarian View of American Education," in Diane Ravitch and Maris Vinovkis, ed., *Learning from the Past: What History Teaches Us About School Reform* (Baltimore and London: Johns Hopkins University Press, 1995), 6.

90 Ravitch, *Left Back*, 348.

91   Paul Gagnon, *Historical Literacy*, 5.

92   Peter Novick, *The Noble Dream: The "Objectivity Question" and the American Historical Profession* (Cambridge: Cambridge University Press), 431; Howard Zinn, *A People's History of the United States: 1492–Present* (New York: HarperPerennial), 686.

93   Ravitch, *Left Back*, 410. In an extensive study in 2003, Abigail and Stephan Thernstrom wrote that the "average black and Hispanic student at the end of high school has academic skills that are at about the eighth-grade level; in fact, on most of the NAEP tests, the majority of black students in twelfth grade have scores Below Basic, while those of Hispanics look only slightly better." See Abigail and Stephan Thernstrom, *No Excuses: Closing the Racial Gap in Learning* (New York: Simon and Schuster, 2003), 22.

94   See http://edexcellence.net/publications/the-state-of-state-us. html. California's standards can be accessed at: http://www.cde. ca.gov/ci/hs/cf/.

95   Quoted in Thernstrom and Thernstrom, *No Excuses*, 25.

96   Ibid.

97   James Loewen, *Lies My Teacher Told Me: Everything Your History Textbook Got Wrong* (New York: Simon and Schuster), 301–302.

98   Congress did establish, in 2001, the Teaching American History (TAH) program. The TAH program has provided millions of dollars in grants to recipients in every state to promote the professional development of teachers of American history. But the results, according to the U.S. Department of Education, have been lackluster. A 2011 report noted that with fewer and fewer states providing statewide history assessments to students it was difficult to measure if students were doing any better because the TAH program. See http://www2.ed.gov/rschstat/eval/teaching/ us-history/tah-report-9-9-11.pdf.

99   The College Board, AP United States History, 21.

100 The College Board, AP United States History, 34–39. An example of a balanced but still sympathetic treatment of American Indians and the Comanche in particular can be seen in S.C. Gwynne, *Empire of the Summer Moon: Quanah Parker and the Rise and Fall of the Comanches, The Most Power Indian Tribe in History* (New York: Scribner, 2010).

101 The College Board, AP United States History, 61.

102 Ibid., 75.

103 Ibid., 79.

104 See http://hnn.us/article/151479.

105 See https://learning.ccsso.org/wp-content/uploads/2022/11/ADA-Compliant-ELA-Standards.pdf.

106 Sandra Stotsky. (2013). Literature or technical manuals: Who should be teaching what, where, and why? Nonpartisan Education Review/Essays, 9 (1). http://nonpartisaneducation.org/Review/Essays/v9n1.htm.

107 http://hnn.us/article/151479.

108 *Federalist 39.*

109 James Otis, "The Rights of the British Colonies" (1764); in Merrill Jensen, ed., *Tracts of the American Revolution* (Indianapolis, 1965), 21.

110 *Federalist 39.*

111 To Joseph Cabell, Feb. 2, 1816; Koch and Peden, eds., *Selected Writings of Jefferson*, 603–604.

112 See https://www.shankerinstitute.org/resource/educating-democracy-state-standards-ensure-civic-core.

113 *Notes on the State of Virginia* (1782), 204.

CHAPTER 4

114 "Panel Faults 'Inadequate' History Curriculums," New York Times, September 30, 1988. http://www.nytimes.com/1988/09/30/us/panel-faults-inadequate-history-curriculums.html.

115 See Finn's introduction to James Leming, Lucien Ellington and Kathleen Porter, edited, Where did Social Studies Go Wrong? (Upper Marlboro: Thomas B. Fordham Foundation, 2003), III–IV.

116 Sheldon Stern and Jeremy Stern, "The State of State U.S. History Standards: 2011" at https://edexcellence.net/publications/the-state-of-state-us.html.

117 David McCullough, *John Adams* (New York: Simon and Schuster, 2001), 163.

118 McCullough, *John Adams*, 70 and 103.

119 King's I Have a Dream Speech is contained in James M. Washington, *The Essential Writings and Speeches of Martin Luther King, Jr.* (New York: HarperCollins, 1991), 217–220.

120 King's Selma speech is contained in Clayborne Carson, David Garrow, Gerald Gill, Vincent Harding and Darlene Clark Hine, *The Eyes on the Prize Civil Rights Reader: Documents, Speeches, and Firsthand Accounts from the Black Freedom Struggle* (New York: Penguin Books, 1991), 224–227.

121 See http://archive.boston.com/news/nation/articles/2011/06/15/students_grasp_of_us_history_lags.

122 See http://www.realclearpolitics.com/Commentary/com-4_18_05_DM.html.

123 The State of the State U.S. History Standards 2011, Massachusetts, The Fordham Institute, 77. See http://www.edexcellencemedia.net/publications/2011/20110216_SOSHS/SOSS_USHistory_Massachusetts.pdf.

124 Ravitch, Diane; *The Language Police: How Pressure Groups Restrict What Children Learn*; Vintage Books, 2004.

125 Fordham study, 78.

126 Anders Lewis is a coauthor of this chapter. From 2001 to 2005 he worked for the Massachusetts Department of Education, serving as a main writer of the 2003 Framework and a facilitator of the curriculum development process.

127 Telephone interview with Anders Lewis, July 27, 2016.

128 Ibid.

129 Telephone interview with Sandra Stotsky, July 21, 2016.

130 Lewis telephone interview.

131 "New York State K–12 Social Studies Framework," Introduction, New York State Education Department, pg. 2. See https://www.nysed.gov/curriculum-instruction/engageny.

132 Ibid.

133 "The State of State U.S. History Standards 2011," 108, The Fordham Institute, http://www.edexcellencemedia.net/publications/2011/20110216_SOSHS/SOSS_USHistory_NewYork.pdf.

134 Patrick Wall, "As social studies overhaul looms, state hopes to avoid Common Core mistakes," *Chalkbeat,* March 10, 2014. See http://www.chalkbeat.org/posts/ny/2014/03/10/as-social-studies-overhaul-looms-state-hopes-to-avoid-common-core-mistakes/#.

135 Telephone interview with Steve Goldberg, August 8, 2016.

136 Goldberg telephone interview.

137 Telephone interview with Greg Ahlquist, August 3, 2016.

138 Patrick Wall, "State aims to close Common Core social studies gap with new curriculum," *Chalkbeat,* January 16, 2014. See http://www.chalkbeat.org/posts/ny/2014/01/16/new-york-aims-to-close-common-core-social-studies-gap-with-new-curriculum/#.

139 Background: New York State K–12 Social Studies Framework, EngageNY, see https://www.nysed.gov/curriculum-instruction/engageny.

140 Ibid.

141 Telephone interview with Kenneth McDonald, August 15, 2016.

142 California History–Social Science Framework 2016, Chapter 1, Introduction, 4. http://www.cde.ca.gov/ci/hs/cf/sbedrafthssfw.asp.

143 Ibid.

144 The State of State U.S. History Standards 2011, Fordham Institute, California, 30. http://www.edexcellencemedia.net/publications/2011/20110216_SOSHS/SOSS_USHistory_California.pdf.

145 Bill Evers, "New school history framework is unhistorical," *The Orange County Register,* April 8, 2016. http://www.ocregister.com/articles/framework-711238-new-ideological.html.

146 Stanley Kurtz, "Will California's Leftist K–12 Curriculum Go National?" *The National Review,* June 1, 2016.

147 Ibid.

148 Curriculum Frameworks Adoption Process, California Department of Education, http://www.cde.ca.gov/ci/cr/cf/cefcfadoptprocess.asp.

149 McDonald telephone interview.

150 Elliott, Scott; "The basics of Indiana academic standards: A new beginning," Chalkbeat, September 8, 2014. See http://www.chalkbeat.org/posts/in/2014/09/08/the-basics-of-indiana-academic-standards-a-new-beginning/#.V5_2zzXCeok.

151 Weddle, Eric; "How Common Core Disintegrated in Indiana," IndyStar, March 30, 2014. See http://www.indystar.com/story/news/education/2014/03/29/common-core-disintegrated-indiana/7051891/.

152 Elliott, Chalkbeat.

153 Banchero, Stephanie; "Indiana Drops Common Core," *The Wall Street Journal*, Aug. 20, 2014. See http://www.wsj.com/articles/indiana-drops-common-core-1395700559.

154 Email from Bruce Blomberg, August 2, 2016.

155 Telephone interview with Bruce Blomberg, July 22, 2016.

156 Blomberg telephone interview.

157 Ibid.

158 "The State of State History Standards 2011," Fordham Institute. See http://www.edexcellencemedia.net/publications/2011/20110216_SOSHS/SOSS_USHistory_SouthCarolina.pdf.

159 South Carolina Social Studies Academic Standards, state board-approved document, August 18, 2011, introduction, 1–2.

160 Telephone interview with Lewis Huffman, former education associate in social studies at the South Carolina Department of Education, July 14, 2016.

161 Ibid.

162 South Carolina Social Studies Academic Standards, Social Studies Standard Page Format, 5.

163 Huffman phone interview.

164 South Carolina Social Studies Academic Standards, Social Studies Standard Page Format, 5.

165 2010 Alabama Course of Study: Social Studies, 4.

166 The State of State U.S. History Standards 2011, Alabama, 20.

167 Telephone interview with Chasidy White, August 8, 2016.

168 Ibid.

169 The authors would like to thank Will Fitzhugh, the editor of *The Concord Review,* for our last two recommendations.

170 This is not to suggest that the 2003 Massachusetts Curriculum could not be improved. The 2003 Massachusetts Framework could use a few revisions to existing standards. For example, U.S. history standard II.4 asks students to "Analyze the causes of the continuing westward expansion of the American people after the Civil War and the impact of this migration on the Indians." Unlike other standards, this standard does not provide any examples. The epic Battle of Little Big Horn, the career of George Armstrong Custer, the life and ideas of Sitting Bull, the decline

of the buffalo, and the massacre at Wounded Knee are a few examples that should be included.

171 David McCullough, "Knowing History and Knowing Who We Are." See http://www.realclearpolitics.com/Commentary/com-4_18_05_DM.html.

CHAPTER 6

172 Daniel J. Singal, "The Other Crisis in American Education," *The Atlantic Monthly,* Nov. 1991, see https://www.theatlantic.com/past/docs/politics/educatio/singalf.htm, 8.

173 Emmett McGroarty, Jane Robbins, & Erin Tuttle, *Deconstructing the Administrative State: The Fight for Liberty*, Manchester, NH: Sophia Institute Press (2017), 100–103.

174 Ralph Ketcham, Anders Lewis, & Sandra Stotsky, *Imperiling the Republic: The Fate of U.S. History Instruction Under Common Core,* Pioneer Institute, No. 121 (Sept. 2014), *available at* https:// pioneerinstitute.org/featured/study-common-core-ela-standardswill-further-harm-u-s-history-instruction/, 13.

175 Howard Zinn, *A People's History of the United States* (New York: HarperPerennial (1980), 686.

176 Kelly King & Sasha Zucker, "Curriculum Narrowing," Pearson Education, Inc. (Aug. 2005), see http://images.pearsonassessments.com/images/tmrs/tmrs_rg/Curriculum Narrowing.pdf.

177 Ketcham *et al., supra* note 10.

178 Diane Ravitch, quoting Will Fitzhugh, "Will Fitzhugh: Common Core, Close Reading, and the Death of History in the Schools," *Education Views*, March 16, 2018, 22–23.

179 Ibid, 23.

180 See, e.g., Stanley Kurtz, "Appalling APUSH: Read It Yourself," *National Review*, Aug. 31, 2014, see https://www. nationalreview.com/corner/appalling-apush-read-it-yourselfstanley-kurtz/.

181 Stanley Kurtz, "Sorry, Still No American Exceptionalism in APUSH," *National Review*, Aug. 3, 2015, see https:// no-americanexceptionalism-apush-stanley-kurtz/.

182 Sheldon Stern, *Effective State Standards for U.S. History: A 2003 Report Card*, Fordham Institute (2003), see https://edexcellence.net/publications/effectivestatehistory.html, 15.

183 Alexander James Inglis, *The Rise of the High School in Massachusetts*, New York: Teachers College (1911), 72–73.

184 Diane Ravitch, "The Plight of History in Schools," in Paul Gagnon, ed., *Historical Literacy: The Case for History in American Education*, Boston: Houghton Mifflin (1989), 61; Diane Ravitch, "A Brief History of Social Studies," in Leming, Ellington, & Porter, *supra* note 3, at 2–3; Diane Ravitch, *Left Back: A Century of Failed School Reforms,* New York: Simon and Schuster (2000), 123–27.

185 See https://malegislature.gov/Laws/GeneralLaws/PartI/TitleXII / Chapter69/Section1D.

186 Massachusetts Framework 1991, 13–14.

187 Massachusetts History and Science Curriculum Framework, 2003, 10–11.

188 Ibid, 12.

189 "The State of U.S. History Standards 2011," Thomas B. Fordham Institute, see https://fordhaminstitute.org/national/research/ state-state-us-history-standards-2011.

190 February 2009 Massachusetts Board of Education minutes see https://archives.lib.state.ma.us/handle/2452/39094.

191 David Randall, *Making Citizens: How American Universities Teach Civics*, National Association of Scholars: New York (2017), see https://www.nas.org/images/documents/NAS_ makingCitizens_fullReport.pdf.

192 Massachusetts Definition of College and Career Readiness and Civic Preparation (2016), 3, see https://www.doe.mass.edu/ccte/.

193 CEPS Certificate Courses by Department Spring List November 2017, Civic Engagement & Service Learning, University of Massachusetts, Amherst, *available at* https://www.umass.edu/ cesl/ sites/default/files/sp_18_content_area_ce_sl_list.pdf.

194 See http://www.doe.mass.edu/bese/docs/FY2018/2017-11/item8a. html.

195 Paul R. Gross and Ze'ev Wurman, *"What Goes Up Must Come Down": New, Lower K–12 Science Standards for Massachusetts,* Pioneer Institute White Paper No. 160 (2016); Mark Bauerlein, R. James Milgram, & Jane Robbins, *Mediocrity 2.0: Massachusetts Rebrands Common Core ELA & Math,* Pioneer Institute, White Paper No. 174 (2017).

196 2018 Revision, 61.

197 2018 Revision, 52–57.

198 2018 Revision, 79–86.

199 2003 Framework, 12.

200 2018 Revision, 4.

201 For example, 2003 Framework, 45; 2018 Revision, 66.

202 For example, 2018 Revision, 42–43.

203 2003 Framework, 47, 52; 2018 Revision, 114.

204 2003 Framework, 61; 2018 Revision, 124.

205 2003 Framework, 74; 2018 Revision, 99.

206 2003 Framework, 75.

207 2018 Revision, 103–104.

208 2018 Revision, 42–45.

209 2018 Revision, 80.

210 2018 Revision, 108–110.

211 2018 Revision, 120. For the complicated nature of the subject, *see* Gregory Clark and Neil Cummins, "Inequality and social mobility in the era of the industrial revolution," in *The Cambridge Economic History of Modern Britain, Volume I: 1700–1870*, eds. Roderick Floud, Jane Humphries, & Paul Johnson, Cambridge University Press: Cambridge (2014), 211–36.

212 2018 Revision, 80.

213 2018 Revision, 104.

214 2018 Revision, 47–48, 63–65; e.g., David Reich, *Who We Are and How We Got Here: Ancient DNA and the New Science of the Human Past*, Pantheon Books: New York (2018).

215 2018 Revision, 82.

216 2018 Revision, 83; and *see* Randy E. Barnett, *Restoring the Lost Constitution: The Presumption of Liberty*, Princeton University Press: Princeton and Oxford (2004).

217 2018 Revision, 57.

218 2003 Framework, 33–47; 2018 Revision, 62–77.

219 2003 Framework, 48–89; 2018 Revision, 90–148.

220 2018 Revision, *passim*; e.g., 146–48.

221 For example, compare and contrast the standards for teaching World War II: 2003 Framework, 76 [USII.15]; 2018 Revision, 105–06 [USII.25–29].

222 2003 Framework, 92–100.

223 2018 Revision, 175–82.

224 2003 Framework, 12; 2018 Revision, 29–30. 39–40, 58–59, 87–89, 143–48.

225 These recommendations echo the spirit, and sometimes the details, of the recommendations in Anders Lewis & William Donovan, *Laboratories of Democracy: How States Get Excellent K–12 U.S. History Standards*, Pioneer Institute, White Paper No. 162 (2017), 20–21.

226 For grave flaws in the College Board's Advanced Placement History examinations, see Peter W. Wood, "The College Board's Modified, Limited Hang Out," National Association of Scholars, September 11, 2015, see https://www.nas.org/articles/Re-re-rerevising_American_History; and David Randall, "Churchill In, Columbus Still Out: A Half-Loaf from the College Board," National Association of Scholars (December 5, 2017), see https://www.nas.org/articles/churchill_in_columbus_still_out_a_half_loaf_from_the_college_board. For equally grave flaws in Common Core history instruction, *see* Ketcham, Lewis, & Stotsky, *supra* note 10.

227 Wilfred M. McClay, "Reunifying History in the Age of Fracture," January 25, 2018, see https://www.proquest.com/openview/a062f21e5df7eadbf5669d3aeb610ed3/1?pq-origsite=gscholar&cbl=54147.

CHAPTER 7

228 "About CSAC," website of the Center for the Study of the American Constitution, see http://csac.history.wisc.edu/aboutus.htm.

229 Ibid.

230 "We the People State Programs, website of We the People, see https://www.civiced.org/we-the-people.

231 *"U.S. Department of Education Awards $50 Million to Support Great Teaching and School Leadership,"* U.S. Department of Education press release, Oct. 5, 2015.

232 Ibid.

233 See *"High School Students' Acquisition of Civic Knowledge: The Impact of We the People,"* Diana Owen, Georgetown University, May 2015. https://www.civiced.org/pdfs/research/ImpactofWethePeople_DianaOwen.pdf.

234 For an understanding of the Massachusetts state hearing questions, see the website of the Center for Collaborative Education at https://www.civiced.org/we-the-people/hearing-questions.

235 Roger Desrosiers, telephone interview, August 17, 2015.

236 Robert Leming, telephone interview, October 26, 2015.

237 Jennifer Patja Howell, deputy director of the Center for the Constitution, telephone interview, Oct. 1, 2015.

238 Robert H. Smith Center for the Constitution, James Madison's Montpelier, see https://www.montpelier.org/center.

239 Emily Voss, outreach and education manager at James Madison's Montpelier, telephone interview, August 14, 2015.

240 Ibid.

241 Howell, telephone interview.

242 Jason Ross, senior director, The Ashbrook Center, telephone interview, September 15, 2015.

243 "TeachingAmericanHistory.org, Seminars and Forums, The Ashbrook Center, see https://teachingamericanhistory.org/.

244 Ibid.

245 Ibid.

246 Ross, telephone interview.

247 Ibid.

248 Ibid.

249 "Rediscovering America," see https://teachingamericanhistory.org/.

250 Ibid.

251 See https://www.washingtonpost.com/lifestyle/magazine/former-supreme-court-justice-sandra-day-oconnor-on-the-importance-of-civics-education/2012/04/10/gIQA8aUnCT_story.html.

CHAPTER 8

252 *Pedagogy Companion to the EAD Roadmap,* https://
www.educatingforamericandemocracy.org/wp-content/
uploads/2021/02/Pedagogy-Companion-to-the-EAD-Roadmap.
pdf, 17–18.

253 The Problem, https://generationcitizen.org/about-us/the-
problem/; The Solution, https://generationcitizen.org/about-us/
the-solutionaction-civics/.

254 A managerial-therapeutic regime replaces free, self-reliant
citizens with subjects ruled by a managerial bureaucracy tasked
not only with determining the country's political and social
policy but also with defining and providing each individual's
happiness. The bureaucrats who suppress free speech on the
grounds that it "causes emotional harm" are the vanguard of the
managerial-therapeutic regime. Paul Edward Gottfried, *After
Liberalism: Mass Democracy in the Managerial State* (Princeton:
Princeton University Press, 1999).

255 Tufts Civic Semester, Jonathan M. Tisch College of Civic Life,
https://tischcollege.tufts.edu/education/tufts-civic-semester.

256 Frederick Hess, "Reimagining Civic Education for the Digital
Age," *Education Next,* July 29, 2020, https://www.educationnext.
org/reimagining-civic-education-for-the-digital-age-icivics/.

257 Games Page, https://www.icivics.org/games.

258 Lesson Plans, https://www.icivics.org/teachers?f[0]=content_
type:lesson_plan.

259 County Solutions Civic Action Plan, iCivics, https://www.icivics.
org/curriculum/countysolutions.

260 Support at iCivics to David Randall, August 9, 2021.

261 Generation Citizen, https://generationcitizen.org.

262 The Problem, https://generationcitizen.org/about-us/the-
problem/; The Solution, https://generationcitizen.org/about-us/
the-solutionaction-civics/.

263 Generation Citizen, *Returning to Our Roots, Educating for
Democracy: A Concept Pater on Youth Civic Engagement,* https://
generationcitizen.org/wp-content/uploads/2016/03/FINAL-
Educating-for-Democracy-11.16.15.pdf.

264 Khin Mai Aung and Greg Fredricks, "Advocacy Within the School House," *The Forge: Organizing Strategy and Practice*, August 19, 2021, https://forgeorganizing.org/article/advocacy-within-schoolhouse?mc_cid=03d19e5ad9&mc_eid=307309a0b5.

265 Vote16USA, https://generationcitizen.org/policy-and-advocacy/vote16usa/.

266 Thomas K. Lindsay and Lucy Meckler, *"Action Civics," "New Civics," "Civic Engagement," and "Project-Based Civics": Advances in Civic Education?* (Texas Public Policy Foundation, 2020), 13–14.

267 The 1619 Project Curriculum, https://pulitzercenter.org/lessonplan-grouping/1619-project-curriculum.

268 Peter Wood, *1620: A Critical Response to the 1619 Project* (New York: Encounter Books, 2020).

269 Share Your 1619 Curricula and Explore Lessons by Other Educators, https://pulitzercenter.org/builder/lesson/share-your1619-curricula-and-explore-lessons-other-educators.

270 Curricular Materials for The 1857 Project, https://pulitzercenter.org/builder/lesson/curricular-materials-1857-project.

271 The 1619 Project Law School Initiative, https://pulitzercenter.org/lesson-plan-grouping/1619-project-law-school-initiative.

272 About BRI, https://billofrightsinstitute.org/about-bri.

273 Yearlong Civics Course, https://billofrightsinstitute.org/yearlongcivics-course; Life, Liberty, and the Pursuit of Happiness, https:// billofrightsinstitute.org/life-liberty-happiness.

274 Core Knowledge, https://www.coreknowledge.org.

275 Civics and CKHG, https://www.coreknowledge.org/curriculum/history-geography/civics-and-ckhg/.

276 The President's Advisory 1776 Commission, *The 1776 Report*, https://trumpwhitehouse.archives.gov/wp-content/ uploads/2021/01/The-Presidents-Advisory-1776-CommissionFinal-Report.pdf.

277 *The Hillsdale 1776 Curriculum: Brutus, Essay XI* (1788), excerpt; John C. Calhoun, *On the Reception of Abolition Petitions* (1837), excerpt; Stephen Douglas, *Speech at Chicago* (1858), excerpt; Roger Taney, *Dred Scott v. Sandford* (1857), excerpt.

278 Ashbrook Center, https://ashbrook.org/about/.

279 About Us, Jack Miller Center, https://jackmillercenter.org/aboutus/#our-mission.

280 Civics Program for Teachers, Lake Forest College, https://www. lakeforest.edu/academics/majors-and-minors/master-of-liberalstudies/civics-program-for-teachers.

281 Stanley Kurtz, "Ultra-Woke Illinois Mandates Are Top Threat to U.S. Education," *National Review,* January 19, 2021, https://www. nationalreview.com/corner/ultra-woke-illinois-mandates-are-topthreat-to-u-s-education/.

282 1776 Unites, https://1776unites.com.

283 The FAIRstory Curriculum, https://www.fairforall.org; Lesson Plans, https://www.fairstory.org/curriculum/lesson-plans/.

284 The Gilder Lehrman Institute of American History, https://www. gilderlehrman.org.

285 Proposed K–12 Civics and Government Standards, https://www. fldoe.org/core/fileparse.php/18736/urlt/CivicsGovernment.pdf.

286 Classic Learning Initiatives, see https://www.cltexam.com.

287 Robert Fenster, "Paid to Sit Through 30 Days of Right-Wing Dogma," *Fenster on Education*, February 27, 2020, https:// fensteroneducation.home.blog/2020/02/27/paid-to-sit-through30-days-of-right-wing-dogma/toolkits/.

Made in the USA
Monee, IL
26 October 2023

45250989R00116